Dr Russell Razzaque is a L
sixteen years' experience
has worked for a number c
organizations during his ca
of Cambridge, the UK Ho
of Justice, and he curren. , ... acute mental
health services in the NHS in east London. He is also
a published author in human psychology with several
books on the subject, and he writes columns for a
number of publications including *Psychology Today*, *The
Independent*, *The Guardian* and *USA Today*.

This book is dedicated to all those I have worked and grown with over the years. Though traditionally defined as doctor and patient, we have, in fact, been assisting each other all along in this journey of mutual awakening we call life.

BREAKING DOWN IS WAKING UP

Can psychological suffering be a spiritual gateway?

Dr Russell Razzaque

WATKINS PUBLISHING

LONDON

This edition published in the UK and Ireland 2014 by
Watkins Publishing Limited
PO Box 883
Oxford
OX1 9PL
UK

A member of Osprey Group

enquiries@watkinspublishing.co.uk

1 3 5 7 9 10 8 6 4 2

Edited and typeset by Donald Sommerville

Printed and bound by CPI Group (UK) Ltd, Croydon, CR0 4YY

A CIP record for this book is available from the British Library

ISBN: 978-1-78028-666-2

Watkins Publishing is supporting the Woodland Trust, the UK's
leading woodland conservation charity, by funding tree-planting
initiatives and woodland maintenance.

www.watkinspublishing.co.uk

Contents

Introduction

EVERYONE NEEDS A BANISTER; a fixed point of reference from which we understand and engage with life. We need something to hold on to, so that when we're hit by life's inevitable disappointments, pain or traumas, we won't fall too far into confusion, despair or hopelessness. With a weak banister we risk getting knocked off course, losing our bearings and falling prey to stress, psychological turmoil and mental illness. A strong banister will stand the test of time in an ever-changing world, giving us more confidence to face the knocks and hardships of life more readily.

Understanding who we are and how we fit into the world is a quest we start at birth and continue through the whole of our lives. Sometimes these questions come to the fore, but usually they bubble away somewhere beneath the surface: 'Who am I?' 'Am I normal?' 'Why am I here?' 'Is there any real point to life?' Deep down inside we know that nothing lasts – the trees, landscapes and life around us will all one day perish, just as surely as we ourselves will, and everyone we know too. But we have evolved ways to hold this reality – and the questions it hurls up – at bay.

We construct banisters to help us navigate our way round this maze of pain and insecurity: a set of beliefs and lifestyles that help us form a concrete context to make sense of things and, as the saying goes, 'keep calm and carry on'. But, for most of us, the core beliefs and lifestyles that hold us together still leave us vulnerable to instability. The sense of identity we evolve is so precarious that we're often buffeted by life onto shaky ground. And, as a consequence, we become prone to various forms of psychological distress; indeed, for vast swathes of society this proceeds all the way to mental illness – whether that be labelled as anxiety, depression, bipolar disorder or the most severe form of mental illness, psychosis.

There are as many types of mental illness as there are people who suffer them. One of the reasons I decided to specialize in psychiatry, shortly after qualifying from medical school, was that, unlike any other branch of medicine, no two people I saw ever came to me with the same issues. Although different presentations might loosely fit into different categories, there appeared to me to be as many ways of becoming mentally unwell as there were ways of being human. I have since specialized in the more severe and acute end of psychiatry – I currently work in a secure, intensive-care facility – but to this day, in 16 years of practice, I have never seen two cases that were exactly the same. And the numbers just seem to be going up. In the UK today, one in four adults experiences at least one diagnosable mental health problem in any one year. In the USA, the figure is the same and this equates to just over 20 million people experiencing depression and 2.4 million diagnosed with schizophrenia, a severe form of mental illness where the individual experiences major disturbances in thoughts and perceptions. The World Health Organization estimates that approximately 450 million people world-wide have a mental health problem.

Beyond these figures, however, are all the people who struggle with various levels of stress throughout life and, all the while, carry a fear at the back of their minds, that they too may one day slide into mental illness. In my experience, this is a fear that pervades virtually every stratum of society. Rarely am I introduced as a psychiatrist to new people in a social gathering without at least some of them quietly feeling, or even explicitly reporting, that they worry that one day they are going to need my help. Such comments are often made in jest, but the genuine anxiety that underlies them is rarely far beneath the surface. There is a niggling worry at the back of many people's minds that something might be wrong with them; that something isn't quite right. What they don't realize, however, in their own private suffering, is just how much company they have in this fear. Indeed, I include myself and my colleagues among them, too. None of us is immune from the existential worry that nags away in the back of our mind.

But, if we look closely, there is also another process that can be discerned underneath all of this. Deep down inside every bubbling cauldron of insecurity, we can also find the seeds of a kind of liberation. Something is just waiting to burst forth. This something is hard to define or describe in language, but it is often in our darkest hours that we can feel it the most. And the further we fall the closer to it we get. This is why, I believe, mental illness can be so powerful, not just because of the deep distress that it contains, but also because of the authentic potential that it represents.

Mental illness, however, is just one aspect of a continuum we are all on. All of us have different ways of reacting emotionally to the experiences we encounter in life and the ones that involve a high level of distress – either for oneself or for others – are the ones we choose to label as mental illness. And it is this end of the spectrum that I will focus on most in this book, as it is these most stark forms of distress that present us with the greatest opportunity to observe the seeds within, and thus, ultimately, learn what is in all of us too.

There may be a variety of factors that contribute to the various forms of mental illness, of course, from childhood traumas to one's genetic make up, but as the cut-off point always centres around distress – which is grounded in subjective experience – the definition itself will always remain somewhat arbitrary. That's not to say that such definitions have no utility. By helping us communicate with each other about these complex shapes of suffering, they will also help us communicate our ideas with one another about how to help reduce the suffering encountered. That is why I use these terms in this book, but it should be noted that I attach this large caveat from the outset. Ultimately, the only person who can really describe a person's suffering is the sufferer himself; outside that individual, the rest of us are always necessarily off the mark. What must invariably be remembered, however, is that there is no 'them' and 'us'. We are all vulnerable to emotional and psychological turmoil in our lives and there is something fundamental about the human condition that makes it so. That is why I believe, as a psychiatrist, that the best research I ever engage in is when I explore my own vulnerabilities. That is when I start to connect with threads of the suffering that my patients are undergoing too. And what I find particularly fascinating about this process is that the deeper I descend into my own world of emotional insecurity, the more I grow to appreciate an indescribable dimension to reality that so many of my patients talk about in spiritual terms, engage with, and indeed rely upon so much of the time.

In a survey of just under 7,500 people, published in early 2013, researchers from University College London found a strong correlation between people suffering mental illness and those with a spiritual perspective on life. Though the results confused many, to me they made perfect sense. There is something at the core of the experience of mental illness that draws sufferers towards the spiritual. Their suffering is an echo of the suffering we all contain within us.

That is why I can say from the outset, and without reticence, that my insights are based largely on a subjective pathway to our shared inner world. And it is through this perspective that I have evolved what I believe is a new banister: a new way of seeing the world and being within in. It is, however, not just that my introspection has taught me about my patients, but that my patients have also taught me about myself. Indeed I can safely say that I have gleaned just as much from the individuals I have cared for as I have from the professionals and teachers I have learnt from. I consider myself hugely lucky to work in a profession in which looking into myself and learning about my own inner world has been, and continues to be, a vital requirement of my work (though, it has to be said that, sadly, many within my profession do not recognize this). It has propelled me into a journey of limitless exploration – of both myself and the people I care for – and this has led me to ever deeper understandings of the nature of mental illness, the mind and reality itself. I have drawn upon a diverse array of wisdom along the way, and my journey has ultimately led me to construct a synthesis of modern psychiatry and ancient philosophy; of new scientific findings and old spiritual practices.

But this banister comes with a health warning, as indeed all should. Just as a set of perspectives and insights can be a useful support in times of instability, so too can over-reliance on them become counterproductive. That is why a banister needs to be held lightly. Gripping too tightly to anything in life is a recipe for exhaustion and, consequently, even greater instability.

What we need is a banister that, when held lightly, can allow us to move forward, rather than hold us back. I believe that such an understanding of reality and our place within it actually exists; it is also imperative to our survival as a species. I believe that life's potential is far greater than most of us are ever aware of, and that our limitations are a lot more illusory than we know. In a sense I feel we are all suffering from a form of mental illness – a resistance to the realization of our true nature – and to that end I humbly offer this book as a guiding rail out of the turmoil.

PART ONE

My Journey

An Exploration of Inner and Outer Worlds

Chapter 1
Wisdom in Bedlam

'One must still have chaos in oneself to be able to give birth to a dancing star.'

Friedrich Nietzsche

MENTAL ILLNESS IS SOMETHING that most of us shy away from. Someone who exhibits behaviour or feelings that are considered out of the ordinary will, sooner or later, experience a fairly broad radius of avoidance around them. Even in psychiatric hospitals this is evident, where the less ill patients will veer away from those who are more unwell. The staff themselves are often prone to such avoidance, too. But contrary to this natural reflex that exists within all of us, moving closer to, and spending time with, someone suffering mental illness can often be quite an enlightening experience. It took me many years to realize this myself, but through the cloud of symptoms, a fascinating display of insight and depth can often be found in even the most acutely unwell. And this turned out to be true whatever the type of mental illness. The problem might be mood-related – for example, depression or bipolar – or what we term neurotic – like anxiety, panic or post-traumatic stress disorder – or all the way up to the paranoia or hearing voices that we see at the most severe stage of mental illness termed psychosis. Indeed, the more severe the symptoms, the deeper the wisdom that appeared to be contained (though often hidden) within it.

A frequent observation of mine, for example, is just how perceptive the people I treat can be, regardless of the very evident turbulence that is going on inside. It is not uncommon for those who are newly admitted to share with me their impressions of the nursing and other staff on the ward with an uncanny degree of accuracy within only a few days of arrival. They'll sometimes rapidly intuit the diverse array of temperaments, perspectives and personality traits among staff members and so have a feel for who is best to approach, avoid, or even wind up, depending on their mental state and needs at the time. It is likely that this acute sensitivity is one of the initial causes of their mental illness in the first place, but the flip side is that they have also managed to glean a lot about life from their experiences to date. This wisdom is often hidden by the symptoms of their illness, but it lurks there under the surface, often ready to flow out after a little gentle probing. I am frequently struck by the profundity of what I hear from my patients during our sessions – and I often find myself feeding this same wisdom back to them – even when, at the same time, they are undoubtedly experiencing and manifesting a degree of almost indescribable psychological pain.

Most of us spend our lives going to work, earning a salary, feeding our families and perhaps indulging in sport or entertainment at the weekends. Rarely are we able to step back from it all and wonder what the purpose of all this is, or whether or not we have our perspectives right. During the football World Cup one year, a patient told me that he felt such events served a deeper purpose for society, 'It stops us thinking about the plight of the poor around the world.' Events such as this kept us anaesthetized, he believed, so we could avoid confronting the depths of inequality and injustice around the globe, and that would ultimately enable the system that propped up the very corporations who were sponsoring these events to keep going. I had to admit that I had never thought of it that way before.

Compassion is a frequent theme I observe in those suffering mental illness, even though they are usually receiving treatment in a hospital setting because, on some level, they are failing to demonstrate compassion towards either themselves or others. I have often been moved by hearing of an older patient with a more chronic history of mental ill-health – perhaps due to repeated long-term drug use, or failure to engage with therapy – taking the time to approach a younger man, maybe admitted to hospital for the first time, and in effect tell him, 'Don't do what I did, son. Please learn from my mistakes.' There are few moments, I believe, that are more powerfully therapeutic than that.

It is only in the last few years that we have discovered, after trialling a variety of treatments, that one of the most powerful interventions for what are known as the 'negative symptoms' of schizophrenia, is exercise. These negative features relate to a lack of energy, drive, motivation and, often, basic functional activity. Whatever the diagnostic label you choose to put on it, this can often be the most disabling part of such illnesses, and there are hardly any known treatments for it. Although an evidence base has recently evolved around the practice of regular exercise. I never quite understood why this could be until a patient one day put forward a hypothesis to me. It takes you out of your mind, he explained to me. 'You see doc, you can't really describe a press-up. You just do it.' The whirlwinds within could be overcome for a few moments at least, while attention is paid, instead, to the body. Suddenly I realized why going to the gym was the highlight of his week.

A rarely described but key feature of mental illness, therefore, is just how paradoxical it can be, with the same person who is plagued by negative, obsessional or irrational thoughts, also able to demonstrate an acute and perceptive understanding of the people and world around him. It is as if one mental faculty deteriorates, only for another one to branch out somewhere else; or rather, consciousness constricts in one area only to expand in another. There is actually some quite startling experimental evidence to back this up. An interesting study was conducted by neuroscientists at Hannover Medical School in Germany and University College London, Institute of Cognitive Neuroscience. It involved a hollow-mask experiment. Essentially, when we are shown a two-dimensional photograph of a white face mask, it will look exactly the same whether it is pointing outwards – with the convex face towards the camera – or inwards – with the concave inside of the face towards the camera. This is known as the hollow-mask illusion. Such photographs were shown to a sample of control volunteers. Sometimes the face pointed outwards, and sometimes inwards. Almost every time the hollow, inward-pointing concave face was shown to them, they misinterpreted it and reported that they were seeing the outward-pointing face of the mask instead. This mis-categorization of the illusion actually occurred 99% of the time. The same experiment was then performed on a sample of individuals with a diagnosis of schizophrenia. They did not fall for the illusion: 93% of the time, this group was actually correctly able to identify when the photo placed before them was, in fact, an inward-pointing concave mask.

Clearly what we see here is an expansion in perceptual ability compared to normal controls. Data like this has begun to pierce the notion that mental illness is purely a negative or pathological experience. In fact, in this study, it was the normal controls who were less in touch with reality than those with a psychotic illness!

The most interesting aspect of this is that, whether they be suffering neurosis, depression, bipolar or even psychotic disorders, many people actually have some awareness of the fact that they are also somehow connecting, through this process, to a more profound reality that they were - like the rest of us - hitherto ignorant of. The experience might be disconcerting, even acutely frightening, but there is a sense that there is also something restorative about it too; they are rediscovering some roots they, perhaps along with the rest of us, had long forgotten about. One patient put it to me this way, 'I feel like I am waking up. But it's very scary because I feel like I have been regressing at the same time. It's almost as if I needed to go through this in order to wake up.'

This sense of a wider meaning and purpose behind a breakdown is not an uncommon theme among the people I see but it is, nevertheless, so counterintuitive that it continues to halt me in my tracks whenever I encounter it. In psychiatry, for genuinely caring reasons, we are striving to reduce the distress that the people we see are experiencing. That, after all, is the reason we became health-care professionals in the first place: to heal the sick. So our reflex, whenever we see people in any kind of pain, is to remove it. But when one senses that the sufferer himself/herself sees value in the experience then we need to stop and think. So long as they are not a risk to themselves or others, perhaps our usual reflex to extinguish such an experience might lead to the suppression of something that could otherwise have been valuable or even potentially transformative.

I have had many experiences of treating people who, even after a terrible episode of psychotic breakdown, came out the other end saying that this was good for them and that the experience, despite being horrendous, was something they needed to go through. This has some- times been attributed to an expansion of awareness that they felt they needed, and that they believed the illness brought to them. A patient once talked with me about a profound, almost overwhelming, sense of gentleness and warmth he felt when listening to music one evening, just hours before his relapse into psychosis, and as we were talking in the session, he suddenly looked up at me and said, with a mixture of awe and joy on his face, and tears in his eyes, 'Sometimes I feel that there is something out there so beautiful and so much bigger than me, but I just can't handle it.'

Though we will be exploring the whole gamut of psychological distress and mental illness in this book, it is the psychotic experience that usually invokes the greatest stereotype and stigma, and so merits extra attention in this opening chapter. Psychosis is when someone is said to have lost touch with reality, and this may involve hearing voices, seeing things or holding some delusional ideas. The idea that someone suffering psychosis can also be the conduit of genuinely deep wisdom and insight, therefore, surprises most people – even mental-health professionals who might not be familiar with this client group. First-person accounts of this are not easy to find in the academic literature, but one particularly good case study was published by David Lukoff in the *Journal of Transpersonal Psychology*. He wrote it in conjunction with a gentleman who had himself suffered a psychotic breakdown and went by the pseudonym of Howard Everest. Howard was able, in a very articulate way, to describe his own breakdown – which he referred to as a form of personal odyssey – both during and after it actually happened.

In the midst of the crisis he remembered thinking, 'This is it. This is the peak. Now it is complete. I am beyond . . . I am the entire circle and all within. There are no longer limitations. I am no longer contained within the frame of my body or my symbols.' He recalled a point, around the time of his hospitalization when, 'I entered a new dimension of the odyssey. One beyond symbols and words.'

He narrated his own anguish and turmoil and the incomprehensibility – to the outside world – of much of his thought processes at the time, yet, similar to a number of my own patients, Howard went on to describe how he believes that the experience was something he ultimately benefited from:

> I have gained much from this experience. With the dawning of a new vision of life has come a new sense of purpose. From a state of existential nausea, my soul now knows itself as part of the cosmos. Each year brings an ever increasing sense of contentment.

Howard felt himself to be more aware after his episode and started to engage in spiritual pursuits such as voluntary work for a church:

> I harbour no resentments towards the psychiatric institution for not taking my 'insights' seriously. I know they were only trying to return me to 'normalcy' the best way they could. I do feel that a great opportunity was lost for them. If they could have seen beyond 'the ravings of a mad man' they might have found something of real value . . . From my perspective the odyssey was a success and I do not regret the experience in any way.

Whether one is inclined towards the spiritual or not, from a purely scientific perspective it should be incumbent upon us in the healing professions to explore claims such as these properly, rather than dismiss them out of hand. Could there actually be something positive and transformative in the experience of mental illness itself?

The idea of an illness sometimes being good for you may sound paradoxical but it isn't entirely alien to us in modern medicine. After all, in the realm of physical health it is well known that exposure to certain illnesses, like infections for example, can be beneficial, helping to strengthen immunity in the long term. This is, of course, the very basis of vaccination. There are also a host of clinical scenarios in which too aggressive an attempt to cure a problem can actually worsen it. This applies with pain medication, for instance, where an over-reliance on pills can lead the body to become tolerant to the analgesia and even ultimately more prone to experiencing pain as a result. This can lead to the sufferer becoming dependant on the painkiller just to stay pain-free. A little closer to home, we see exactly the same picture with drug treatments for sleep problems. In the UK doctors are advised to prescribe them as infrequently as possible, and never more than 28 days at a time, for fear, paradoxically, of making the insomnia worse than it was in the first place. Some non-pharmacological treatments for insomnia actually involve exposure to sleeplessness in order to help the body find its own balance.

Could something similar be happening in mental illness? There is no doubt, of course, that mental illness can be a devastating and intolerable experience for many, often necessitating urgent treatment, but could there also be occasions when actual exposure to the illness itself functions as a deeper level cure? Might there be some genuine validity to what some of these sufferers have been saying about the positive aspects of their experience? And if this is the case, then what are those positive aspects and what is the underlying problem or dysfunction that is being rectified? And how might this sometimes amount to a personal transformation?

I had been asking myself these questions for a number of years, but it was ultimately only through my own journey of inner exploration and personal development that I began to find some answers . . .

Chapter 2
Parallel Pathways

'When we remember that we are all mad,
the mysteries of life disappear and life
stands explained.'

Mark Twain

IT HAD BEEN A PARTICULARLY DIFFICULT couple of years
in my personal life and professionally the heat was also
on, with a number of crucial exams coming up that I
needed to pass in order to take my career to the next
level. Someone recommended a meditation retreat to
me and, without putting much thought into it, I booked
myself onto a weekend down in Devon from Friday
night to Sunday afternoon. It was an idyllic location
known as Gaia House, a mindfulness meditation centre
set amongst some of the most beautiful rolling country-
side England has to offer. It was billed as a pathway to
relaxation and inner peace and so I found myself arriving
with a host of city-dwellers like me longing for some quiet
serenity and country air. The minute I arrived, however,
I realized that I was in for a very different experience
than the one I had imagined.

The organizers described the itinerary for the weekend
– a mixture of meditation sessions, involving walking,

sitting and standing meditation practices with breaks in between – and then, at the end, matter-of-factly, they dropped in the instruction that talking would cease before dinner and would not resume again till Sunday lunchtime. The notion startled me. I realized that I hadn't been silent for that long since I first learned to talk nearly thirty years before. In addition, we were not allowed to watch any television, use our phones or even read any books. This was a silent retreat, something I hadn't realized at the time I signed up.

The first day was anything but relaxing. We were given the simplest of instructions for meditation: just observe your breathing as you sit in silence. If you start thinking about anything, just notice that you are thinking. Observe whatever comes up without getting sucked into it. Just observe.

And what I observed was chaos. A constant whirl of thoughts that I repeatedly had to make an effort to zoom out of, to observe again and again. This kept happening; I was getting sucked back into my thoughts over and over, then pulling myself out again. I felt like a novice swimmer in the middle of a stormy ocean, bobbing perpetually in and out of my waves of thought. And each time I brought myself back out again, I felt like a fool for not being able to keep my mind still for just a minute. It was only when the teacher told us that this was normal, that I started to relax a little. Buddhists refer to this natural tendency with the description 'monkey mind'. That is exactly how mine felt. I had lived with my mind ever since I learnt to talk and think, but I had never realized just how messy and frequently unproductive it was, until I stopped to listen to it for the first time. It was quite a revelation to me, and the whole experience was brought home by a few words from our teacher – a woman by the name of Leela Sarti, whose infinitely serene voice I still remember to this day when she uttered three words that I can honestly say changed my life, 'Thinking is overrated.'

At first the idea struck me as heresy. I was trained to treasure my thinking. From a scientific, medical perspective, thinking was what I believed to be my greatest asset. But the more I actually just sat and observed myself thinking – even when I didn't wish to think about anything – the more I realized how out of my own control my thinking mind actually was.

By the end of the weekend, I realized that the difference between me and my patients was far more subtle than I had understood so far. Yet the very act of spending time shining awareness on the cacophony of thought inside led me to feel more relaxed than I had been for a long time. I returned to work on the Monday genuinely feeling as if I had returned from a three-month break.

That was nearly ten years ago and, since then, many retreats later, I have managed slowly to build up a regular meditation practice. And yet my monkey mind is still there. Only now it is a little quieter and I dance in tune with it a lot less than I used to. But, through the process of observing my own mind in this way, I feel I have come to understand my patients better. Irrelevant and unnecessary thoughts are by no means the preserve of the mentally ill. We all have them going on inside all the time. In fact, the very process of exposing oneself to the endless vicissitudes of one's inner world in this way is not unlike the experience of the anxiety sufferer. Both are experiences of being almost overwhelmed by the stream of thought within; the main difference is that the meditator's experience is a voluntary one, whereas the person experiencing a panic attack, phobia or generalized anxiety is fighting against his experience with all his might. I began to notice that the turmoil my patients with anxiety disorders described when they had an attack sounded a lot like the inner world I watched in myself when I was meditating. The perpetual flow of assumptions, insecurities, fears and judgements was a hallmark of this inner whirlwind. Only I went out of my way to observe this experience internally, whereas they did the opposite – or tried to at least – which paradoxically led to it spilling over. It is only in the last few years that the world of mainstream psychology has been unearthing the profound therapeutic value of acceptance, as opposed to avoidance, when it comes to our inner world of emotions. Opening ourselves up to our experiences, rather than struggling to suppress them, turns out to be a powerful treatment for symptoms of mental illness. I will address this in more detail in later chapters on treatment.

The exposure to my own inner chatter through meditation made me relate better, not just to people with anxiety, but to those with mania too. Terms traditionally used in psychiatry to describe the experience of mania include 'racing thoughts', which is, as the name suggests, a rapid stream of thought; 'flight of ideas', which is an incessant jumping from one topic to another – all linked to each other – but all flowing one into the other, at fast speed; and 'pressure of speech', which is the external verbal manifestation of such a racing mind. Without the external verbal manifestation, the internal experience of barely controllable thought is, again, something that is not at all unfamiliar to the meditator. People often mistake meditation as an instant immersion into peace and tranquillity, like slipping into a warm bath, when, in fact, it is more like paddling around a whirlpool. One who meditates is, therefore, very unlikely to perceive the experience of having racing thoughts or flights of ideas as remotely exotic. Such experiences are indeed the very cornerstone of meditation.

What became clear to me through these early comparisons with anxiety and mania was the way in which much of spiritual practice is, in many respects, a voluntary and conscious exposure to experiences that, when involuntary, unwanted and therefore exaggerated, are actually symptoms of mental illness. It was as if spiritual practitioners and sufferers of mental illness were going through the same process, but mirrored.

I have found this to be the case across a wide variety of psychopathologies. Another common symptom of mental illness observed by psychiatrists is what we call 'psychomotor retardation'. This is when both movement and thought profoundly slow down and activity almost becomes robotic. It is most commonly observed in major depression – sometimes in chronic psychotic illnesses too – and it can result in an impairment of function that might mean the sufferer finds difficulty engaging in the most mundane activities such as bathing or self-care. Simple tasks like writing a cheque, turning on the TV or climbing the stairs might seem almost impossible. Sometimes the sufferer feels unable to perform more than the smallest of movements, or think the simplest of thoughts, narrowing the range of what is possible, which might, in severe cases, even result in becoming bed-bound.

This very slowing down of movement and thought, however, is also a deliberate practice engaged in on spiritual retreats as a way – akin to meditation – of training the 'monkey mind'. It is attempted via a variety of means and exercises, and an excellent description of such practices is provided by the American psychiatrist, Mark Epstein, in his highly acclaimed book *Going On Being*. In it Mark talks about his own introduction to such spiritual practice when he attended the Naropa Institute – a Buddhist summer school – in 1974:

> I was thrown into situations where the spiritual disciplines of the Eastern world were opened up for me. I was amazed at how simple and repetitive they all were. I took a class in the Chinese art of t'ai chi and spent an hour every day practising three movements; lifting my hands softly up to my chest, pulling them into my breastbone, and lowering them with my palms facing outward. I took a yoga class in which I raised my hands over my head, bent down to touch the floor, and raised myself back up to standing over and over again . . . I went to a regular *kirtan*, or devotional singing group, in which we repeated the words 'Sri Ram, Jai Ram' in a call and response with

the leader for hours at a time. I wanted to learn to play a set of Indian drums called the *tabla* but was only allowed to practise one movement with the thumb and forefinger of my right hand. I even took a meditation-inspired dance class in which we walked up and down a forty-foot line of the floor for the duration of each period, making only the smallest of variations in our movements . . .

Years later, when watching the movie *The Karate Kid* with my children, I felt a moment of kinship with the young karate student who is forced, in his first lesson with his Japanese master, to spend his time washing cars, practising the same circular washing movement throughout a seemingly endless day.

Mark goes on to describe the fundamental purpose, from a spiritual perspective, of such apparently inane practices.

The lesson of this first confrontation with spiritual discipline was a profound one for me. Far from being a dead end, these repetitive, boring and stupid practices held the key to the freedom that I was pursuing but could not understand. All of these disciplines threw me back into my own mind; they brought up a host of reactions that I did not want to acknowledge. I was not so patient and accepting as I would have liked to have thought. I was impatient, judgemental and obsessively lost in repetitive thoughts. I could think about the same things over and over again in lieu of being in the moment. The spiritual practices all required me to pay attention to the present, and, if this was not possible, to whatever prevented me from doing so.

We see here again, then, that the same form of mental and physical slowing that can be characteristic of a depressive illness is what is being voluntarily entered into by the spiritual adherent. It is like a deliberate provocation of the mind, a destabilization with the intention of reaching something beyond it. I have engaged in similar practices myself in retreats I have attended, such as walking meditation. Here you walk extremely slowly, consciously and methodically – as opposed to automatically – placing one foot before the other, to reach the end of the room only to turn round and walk back again. This would continue for up to an hour, several times a day. Then, when back at work, I would see people suffering severe depression or psychosis doing exactly the same thing, pacing slowly and deliberately up and down the corridors of the hospital ward.

For me, these were actions that took great effort and will-power to engage in, but those in hospital were making no choice at all. It was their illness, and all the factors that caused it – the losses, the traumas, the inheritance and the hurts – that were driving them to perform these actions.

It is not only Eastern spiritual practices that have parallels in mental illness. Fasting is a common aspect of religious faiths around the world, particularly those in the Abrahamic tradition – Christianity, Judaism and Islam. The people who fast are choosing to abstain from food for religious reasons, but this does not mean that the thought of food is extinguished from their minds. If anything, it is often heightened, and sometimes – just before the breaking of the fast – it becomes a virtual preoccupation. Sometimes it is said that the experience of this very craving is the point of the fast itself. Key features of this – both the practice and the mindset that sometimes underlies it – have resonance with the sufferer of anorexia who is also intentionally denying himself food, not for reasons of suppressed appetite but, if anything, the reverse. In fact, a frequent preoccupation with food is a common feature of the disorder. The main difference from someone who is fasting, of course, is in the motivation. While devout Muslims or Christians may be doing it to further their own spiritual development, the sufferer of anorexia is doing it to lose weight and, as a result, their fast is often prolonged, sometimes with tragic consequences.

There is a broader range of ascetic practices, of course, that are engaged in by monastic orders across all faiths. As well as the limitation of food intake, they will also involve abstinence from sex, long periods of silence, renunciation of material possessions and a degree of disengagement from the wider society. Such a generalized withdrawal from the social world the rest of us live in is also characteristic of severe depression. Here symptoms often include a substantial reduction in diet, lack of sexual activity, lack of interest in work and economic activity in general, whether that be shopping, travelling or even watching TV. In fact, the simplified, electively solitary life of someone with severe depression has many similarities to that of a Buddhist or Christian monk. Again, the monk has made the conscious choice to devote himself to this path, whereas the individual struck by depression has been driven to this lifestyle by a combination of life and genes. It is almost as if they both arrive at similar destinations through very different pathways, one driven by free will and the other by a seeming lack of it.

It is when we look into psychosis, however, that we find the most illuminating intersection between spirituality and mental illness. My most recent trip to Gaia House was for a week-long silent retreat. By now, my regular attendances at Gaia House made me look forward to such retreats more and more. But a week without any talking, TV, books, phones, computers or iPads was still something that evoked a sense of foreboding within. What's more, there were about sixty of us there together this time. We would pass each other and make only fleeting, tentative eye contact in the often narrow corridors. We would listen in silence to the mindfulness lessons delivered by *dharma* teachers – people who had undergone rigorous spiritual training in Buddhist monasteries and now toured the world helping others attain the wisdom of the Buddha's teachings – and then meditate together. We would eat together, and, as part of the training, perform the household chores together, as mindfully as possible. We even slept in the same rooms together. And all in silence. The people who attended were from all walks of life from civil servants to psychologists, business people and lawyers and, though we all spent every waking moment together, none of us knew a thing about anyone else. What's more, none of us knew what anyone else thought about us. I remember becoming insecure about whether or not I had done something wrong or been neglectful or perhaps taken too much food during mealtimes. I worried about how I was coming across and my mind even started to develop mini paranoias. I began to see a little of life through the lenses of my psychotic patients. The volume of my thinking mind was sometimes louder than ever. In between the stillness of meditation, I would find myself loudly internally commenting on my actions and things around me in a similar way to what schizophrenic patients classically experience, in the form of a voice in their heads, commenting on their actions; this is known as a Schneiderian first-rank symptom of schizophrenia.

Unlike the experience of my patients, however, I found myself settling into the environment over time. I gained greatly from the practice by the weekend, and at the end of the retreat when talking resumed, we discovered that most of us shared the same insecurities, paranoias and constantly commenting mind at some point during the retreat. Even those who did not come from a professional mental-health background remarked on how similar they felt their experience might have been to what they had heard or read about schizophrenia.

Somehow the process of our spiritual development was entering similar, even overlapping, territory with that of the acutely mentally ill. It took me back to one of the first things I noticed in my earliest experience of psychiatry, many years ago, namely, the extent to which spiritual concepts appeared to permeate psychosis. Every week there would be an admission of someone who either believed he was talking to God or, indeed, was God. This has been a consistent experience throughout my career. As a measure of just how frequent such intersections are, I did a brief audit on my own ward over a three-month period and found that two-thirds of all our admissions had delusions with a heavily spiritual content. The NHS unit I work on tends to specialize in psychosis and nine out of the twelve admissions we had in that period presented with symptoms centred around spirituality. Below are very brief snippets from some of their presentations. I have, of course, altered names and key information in order to preserve confidentiality:

> Peter became increasingly agitated soon after admission, when he began expressing the belief that he had received instructions from God.

> Steve said, during one review, 'I am blessed. I am everyone. I learn from a flower.' He also said that he hears God and that God laughs with him.

> John said that God was guiding him and supporting him. Later he said that 'Jesus is coming to defend me' and stated that he is the apple of God's eye.

> During my session with Miles, half-way through, he started to smile and wink at 'an angel' who he said was talking to him from the corner of the room.

> Mr O'Hanlon thinks he is Jesus Christ and a Prophet and has psychic abilities.

Joe believes that God talks to him. He wrote letters to his neighbours expressing that he had contact with God. He has asked staff to refer to him as God, believing that he is a God.

Jack believed that he died in 2005. During a review he proclaimed to the doctors, 'Don't you know that I am God? What I say will happen. If I say there will be no injection then there will be no injection.'

Anthony was initially mute most of the time. When he started talking, however, he spoke of seeing visions of God appearing before him.

Such descriptions will be entirely familiar to anyone working in acute psychiatry. This kind of presentation is an everyday experience in psychiatric wards around the world. Community psychiatrists also sometimes manage to see people just prior to a psychotic episode setting in and, here, a particular experience, known as 'delusional atmosphere' can occur. In it, the individual starts to feel that something is about to shift in his perception of reality. There is almost a tangible sense of anticipation that something dramatic is about to change, like the ground is shifting beneath him and some sort of major realignment is occurring. Then, as predicted, and all of a sudden, the person entering into psychosis will break out of the reality paradigm the rest of us reside in. They have approached the borderlands of human consciousness, as it is experienced through our logical minds, and then crashed right through. They appear subsequently to reside in a place that is outside our four walls of ordinary logic and, in describing this experience, a common theme is that of contact with some form of spiritual reality that, they claim, exists beyond normally available human experience.

The way society has attempted to understand such experiences has varied widely throughout our history. It is noteworthy that, for much of our past, individuals undergoing such breaks with reality were actually seen as a source of spiritual wisdom for the community – a wisdom that had been attained through exactly such breakdowns. The eminent psychiatrist Dale Archer in his excellent book *Better Than Normal*, takes a fascinating look into the world of the shaman, whom he describes as 'sacred individuals, the spiritual guides of the Stone Age village'. And what he discovers is a profound series of parallels between them and those we currently diagnose with schizophrenia.

> Shamanic powers tend to originate at puberty, which is the same time that schizophrenic symptoms first start to appear. Shamanic visions are similar to the hallucinations experienced by people with schizophrenia. And the prevalence rate of schizophrenia . . . is about the same as the prevalence of shamans in today's tribal societies.

The journey into psychosis is not only akin to the experience of the shaman. Strong parallels exist with virtually every significant sage in history. Whether it be the Buddha or Jesus Christ, they each were said to have left their regular earthly lives and responsibilities to journey into an unknown realm and face the challenge of deep-seated forces – often described as inner demons. Buddha sat for days under the bodhi tree, just as Jesus spent weeks in the desert, experiencing a period of genuine anguish and turmoil, before ultimately connecting to a divine presence beyond the parameters of any reality they had previously known. After that they returned to their communities to spread the wisdom they had attained through their perilous inner journeys.

Even some of the specific experiences described by these spiritual leaders resonate strongly with common features of psychosis. Buddhism, for example, talks of the experience of *nirvana* being akin to having no self. One's existence is merged with all of creation and so one is no longer a separate individual with a discernible ego. In both depression and schizophrenia-like illnesses, the sufferer can experience what is known as nihilistic delusions where he feels that he, his friends, family and/or other parts of the world no longer exist. Indeed a common characteristic of psychosis is the way in which the lines between self and non-self become significantly blurred, to the point where the sufferer is no longer able to distinguish between her own experiences and those arising from the outside. The very notion of her separate existence somehow seems to be melting away. Yet, this attainment is itself the very objective of the mystic.

Such states of enlightenment are said to be beyond thought itself. Those who have attained enlightenment are said to have transcended the thinking mind, and here again there are clear parallels with psychosis. 'Poverty of thought' is a phenomenon that occurs in people who may have experienced a long-term chronic psychotic illness, and now possess an apparent scarcity of inner mental activity. They are frequently mute and relatively unreactive. When asked questions, they may respond monosyllabically after long pauses. They will engage in few activities, and interactions with others are minimal and perfunctory. Again, like the mystic, they inhabit a world of silence, a world beyond thought.

This connection is so well documented, in fact, that in 2010 the Royal College of Psychiatrists published a book edited by three well-known academic psychiatrists, Chris Cook, Andrew Powell and Andrew Sims, entitled *Spirituality and Psychiatry*. The book consists of an extensive trawl through all the literature published in the field about the nexus between these two realms, and in the chapter on psychosis, by Mitchell and Roberts, they reveal that numerous studies

> ... have found it impossible to differentiate between mystical experiences and psychosis solely on the basis of phenomenological description ... We share the view that there are no clear phenomenological differences that distinguish the psychotic experience from the spiritual one, but that they differ in terms of life consequence.

One of the papers they quote is by Jackson in 2001 – 'Psychotic and spiritual experience: a case study comparison' – which states that many people see their psychosis 'as part of a process through which they reached, from their perspective, a constructive spiritual reorientation'.

In this context, it is entirely understandable, then, that people who have experienced mental illness tend to place spirituality more centrally in their lives than the general public. This, indeed, has been borne out by surveys. One questionnaire, for example, found that 79% of patients rated spirituality as 'very important' to them – a figure that is likely to be many multiples higher than the average for the general population. Again, this is not a statistic that would surprise anyone working in the field of mental health. Requests to see the chaplain are commonplace in psychiatric wards and, whatever their religion, those staying in such facilities frequently look forward to a visit from a priest, imam or other spiritual equivalent.

Recently I have got to know the chaplain allocated to my own ward, a young woman named Mirabai, very well. She is a regular visitor to our unit and, indeed, a session with her is frequently one of the first things people ask for on admission. Consequently, I often find that she is even busier than I am – rushing from one patient to the next – trying to fit them all in during her packed working day. There is a hunger for her to help them make sense of some of the profound experiences they are having, often based on the conviction that there is a definite spiritual dimension to it. Over time I have come to appreciate her as a truly valuable colleague and one of the most important resources we have in our service.

What I never expected, however, is that one day I too would be seeking her counsel to help understand an experience of my own.

Chapter 3
The Signposts Within

'Who looks outside dreams; who looks inside awakens.'

Carl Jung

I WAS BROUGHT UP A MUSLIM. I read the Koran, learnt the tenets of the faith and prayed five times a day. As I grew older and left university, however, my adherence to the prescribed beliefs I was taught in childhood began to wane. I found myself appreciating the elements of my faith that were common with all others, and eventually could no longer consider myself belonging to any one faith over any other. Later on, I experienced a further shift as I began to feel uncomfortable with literal concepts of God, sitting on high, passing judgements on all, and the fixed notions of Heaven and Hell that this entailed. I still had respect for those who chose to follow a religious path – so long as they didn't judge me for not joining them – but I officially started to consider myself an agnostic; although, if I was really being honest with myself, I leaned more towards atheism.

I originally began meditating purely as a means of stress relief and personal psychological development. I wasn't hoping to find any spiritual answers through the process; it was all about enhancing my own self-awareness and so improving my quality of life. I found it difficult, but the fact that I found it so onerous intrigued me. There had to be a lot more going on inside me than I realized if I couldn't just sit still for 15 minutes a day. It became a form of exploration, a kind of self-therapy. I found myself becoming calmer, more open, less judging, better able to handle difficult situations and see issues from many different points of view without necessarily losing my own. All of these changes were of great benefit to me in my role as a psychiatrist and I often found myself wondering if there was a way that my patients could benefit from something similar, too.

It was a number of years, however, before I began to notice mindfulness- and meditation-related therapies cropping up in the mainstream literature. Journals were increasingly publishing studies around such interventions, which emerged through a variety of techniques; from Mindfulness-Based Cognitive Behaviour Therapy (MCBT) to Dialectic Behaviour Therapy (DBT) to Acceptance and Commitment Therapy (ACT), and I excitedly began to study, then apply some of their methods into my own work. ACT was my particular favourite and, after getting to know its founder, Professor Steven Hayes, liaising with and learning from him directly, I started to conduct some trials on ACT-based treatments in my ward – in the form of combined interventions for both staff and patients. I will talk more about these treatments in later chapters of the book, but what this enabled me to do personally was to develop a regular form of meditation practice at work. This meant that I was effectively meditating twice a day, enjoying its benefits ever more deeply, and also seeing it in my patients and colleagues who attended.

Then, one day, as I sat meditating at home, before work, I found myself descending into a deeply meditative state; I somehow travelled through the sensations of my body and the thoughts in my mind to a space of sheer nothingness that felt, at the same time, like it was somehow the womb of everything. I felt a sense of pure power and profound energy as I came upon a sudden brilliant light and a profound feeling of all-pervading joy. To say that I experienced it, however, would be a mischaracterization for there was no sense of me any more. I was the experience itself. And, even though it lasted mere seconds, there was no beginning of it and there was no end of it, because there was no beginning and no end of me. I was everything and nothing at the same time. And when I came out of it, and could feel myself in the room again, a sense of hilarious laughter came upon me, as if I had momentarily awakened from a giant joke I had been playing on myself – pretending to be all these people, creatures and things when, in fact, that was all just make-believe. Like a girl playing with a dolls' house, I'm just playing at being different people, when in fact it's all me. And when I say me, I don't mean Russell Razzaque. That's just another pretend me. I suddenly realized that Shakespeare was right: all the world is indeed a stage. Only it happens to be the same actor playing all the roles.

Even though the experience lasted for no more than a few seconds, it has had a more profound effect on me than any other moment in my life. It has left me feeling a deep sense of connection with everything and everyone around me and, in the first few days afterwards, this sense of connection was so intense that it often felt like I was the same being everywhere, just shape-shifting into different forms. The whole of life and existence felt like a game.

I had recently brought a Kindle and so was able to access books on the subject at the touch of a button, and so I started to read around awakening experiences avidly. As I did, I discovered that millions of people around the world and throughout history have had similar experiences through meditation and related pursuits, or sometimes even just spontaneously. One of the most inspirational contemporary teachers in the West to have written on the subject is a man named Adyashanti. Originally from the San Francisco Bay area, Adyashanti wrote a book about such experiences called *The End of Your World*. In it he wrote a little about his own awakening experience:

> It was an irrevocable and irreversible event, an irreversible seeing. What I saw . . . was that I am everything and nothing, and I also am beyond everything and nothing. I saw what I am is inexpressible. It had the sense of going through and through – right to the very root of existence.

Adyashanti went on to write several books on the subject and has been touring the world fairly regularly since. With his youthful features and unassuming, neighbourly American voice he probably sounds less like a spiritual guru than anyone imaginable, but his insights are indeed profound and they have resonated with so many people that he now has a global following.

The late Eknath Easwaran was another famous writer on the subject. In his book *The Dhammapada* – an introduction and translation of the classic Buddhist text – the former professor of English literature provides another vivid description of the experience:

> When the thought process has been slowed to a crawl in meditation . . . the movie of the mind stops and you get a glimpse right through the mind into deeper consciousness. This is called 'bodhi', and it comes like a blinding glimpse of pure light accompanied by a flood of joy.

An important caveat that goes alongside every such description of awakening, however, is that no permutation of words can ever do it justice. Indeed, every articulation will inevitably be misleading to some degree because, however poetically adroit you might be, the essence, profundity and intensity of the experience can never be captured in language. Something will always be lost in translation, for it is an attempt to describe that which is beyond words with words. There is a good Zen saying about this: 'Don't mistake the finger pointing to the moon for the moon itself.' That is the same caveat I attach to my own description. However hard I worked to construct the perfect prose around my experience, I always knew that I would fail, and you should know that, too. Indeed I thought long and hard about whether or not I should try to describe it at all, but I ultimately decided to because of the experiences that were associated with it, experiences that profoundly shook the way in which I understood mental illness and the suffering of my patients. For the awakening experience comes with a flip side. There is something deeply disorientating about it. Here again, Adyashanti articulates the experience about as well as anyone can:

> Most of what we are told about awakening sounds like a sales pitch for enlightenment. In a sales pitch we are told only the most positive aspects . . . We are told that enlightenment is all about love and ecstasy, compassion and union and a host of other positive experiences . . . One of the most common sales pitches includes describing enlightenment as an experience of bliss. As a result, people think, 'When I spiritually awaken . . . I will enter into a state of constant ecstasy.' This is, of course, a deep misunderstanding of what awakening is . . .
>
> On the contrary, enlightenment may not be easy or positive at all. It is not easy to have our illusions crushed. It is not easy to let go of long held perceptions. We may experience great resistance to seeing through even those illusions that cause us a great amount of pain.

And, indeed, that's how it was with me. Particularly in the early days I felt something deep inside me pulling me in the opposite direction. A resistance to the experience and the processing of it that threatened to throw me off course at times. In those moments I saw all the pathways to the mental states of my patients. It was as if I had reached the event horizon – the term astrophysicists give for the edge of a black hole, the very boundary of time and space as we know it. And, just like an event horizon, my mind was a whirl of activity, fighting to keep a hold of the reality it had been cocooned within all this time. I could sense the powerful currents in my whirling mind – the self-doubts and dents in self-esteem sucking me towards a ball of depression, the anxieties and fears threatening to balloon into full-blown panic, obsessions or defensive compulsions, and the speed of it all that risked pushing me into a manic state. I could feel a cauldron of insecurity on the verge of blowing up onto the world around me, projecting deep-seated fears onto my surroundings, conjuring up demons, conspiracies and the stuff of psychosis. All the potential was there.

Back at work, when patients described experiencing everything around them – the TV, trees, houses and other people – recognizing and talking to them, I felt I could make more sense of their experience than ever before. I could see how this experience of really being one with everything could lead to that, or even to grandiose ideas about one's own divinity or a sense of omnipotence or omniscience.

The books I read on the subject included details of the life of Buddha and how, before his own fully fledged enlightenment, he had to undergo an inner battle with a demon known as Mara. This, in many Buddhist traditions, is recognized as an inner force within the unconscious, rather than a concrete external reality. It is the ego – the separate sense of self – fighting to regain control. The story describes how Mara offered the Buddha all the riches and the power in the world to divert him, and when he refused that, Mara put forward his three temptress daughters to entice the Buddha back to the world of craving and passion. Again the Buddha rejected them. It is a story not unlike that of the temptation of Christ who is said to have spent 40 days and nights in the Judean desert, when the Devil approached him with temptations designed to divert him from his ultimate realization.

Both of these can be seen as powerful metaphors for the inner turmoil that accompanies transitions towards enlightenment. Mara or Satan represent the commenting mind – the inner critic – the aspect of them that wanted to cling on to the material reality they knew. And so, locked in a struggle with their psyches, the Buddha and Christ's experience of enlightenment also shows the simultaneous potential for descent into insanity. I talked my experience through tentatively with a couple of colleagues and their receptivity took me aback. Mirabai, our chaplain, told me that she had exactly such an experience a couple of years before. She described the similar research she did around it herself at the time, and how she learnt about the importance of remaining grounded above all else. She also encouraged me to write down what I had learnt for the benefit of others, particularly coming from someone in my position. On the one hand she reminded me of the importance of maintaining humility while, on the other, warning me to not lose sight of the benefit I could bring to others by articulating my new-found perspectives, especially for the sake of my patients and my profession. Although I would not put pen to paper for many months, it was then that I made the resolution to write this book.

Another person I talked it through with was Diana. She is a doctor on my team who is essentially my deputy. Diana is a psychiatrist I have a great deal of respect for and whose opinion I rely on virtually every working day. Of Romanian origin, she is also a practising Orthodox Christian, but I had no idea how that would play into her interpretation of my experience. Nevertheless, during one of our meetings, I found myself describing it to her. As I began to, I noticed her looking at me intently and, after a while, she appeared to be nodding knowingly. I asked her if she recognized something in my description and she told me that, while she had not had such an experience herself, what I was describing was precisely the experience her church elders went through during their monastic training. Meditation and similar contemplative work was central to the Orthodox perspective – something I hadn't realized – and Diana told me how, through silence, all her church elders were taught to recognize their own connections to what they saw as divine consciousness.

Her account of their experiences again resonated profoundly with my own; she talked of a deep nothingness which was simultaneously filled with an energy, which they believed was a manifestation of Christ. It was through such connections that they evolved their wisdom before going back out into the community to support others in their faith, and she had been brought up on such descriptions of awakening from her childhood. Diana believed that this contemplative dimension was one of the main ways in which her own Orthodox faith was differentiated from Western versions of Christianity.

I told her about the currents that existed at the periphery of this experience that resonated with the mental states of our patients, and this made immediate sense to her, too. She then imparted to me some profound advice, words of wisdom that I find myself coming back to again and again: 'Remember that you are nothing.' This deep humility was the antidote to any helium-like effect that risked carrying me off into the clouds of deeper illusion as a result of the experience I had.

A feeling of being everything and nothing makes no sense whatsoever to the logical mind. That is why, again, the words can never really be used as a genuine guide to the experience itself, but they are the best that we can do. And in the vortex of this paradox we see its dangers. To believe that we are everything takes us down the path of delusion and self-inflation, and to believe that we are nothing takes us down the path of self-denial and ultimately self-destruction. Maintaining awareness of both sides of the experience is, therefore, vital to maintaining balance. But this is not always an easy task.

After the experience, I embarked upon a new stage in my journey. There were clearly parallels between my own experience and those of my patients. There were also clear routes through which my experience could transform into theirs. But I had approached and achieved my experience through very different means. There were also key differences between my experience and theirs and the outcomes were, indeed, profoundly different. I was keen, however, not to dismiss them simplistically as totally unrelated, for they clearly weren't. Understanding how these very similar experiences, with totally different outcomes, fitted together became my mission in the months ahead. I searched, networked, read and wrote, and gradually the pieces started to fall into place. I came to realize that, in the same way, we all possess a vulnerability to mental illness and we also all possess the potential for awakening. In fact, the two go together; one cannot exist without the other. This, to my mind, is the fundamental nature of the human condition. I believe that a better understanding of this process – through the prism of psychiatry – could be of genuine value to society, as well as those afflicted by mental illness and their relatives, and that is what I will lay out through the remaining sections of this book.

PART TWO

Know Thyself

The Mystery of Reality

Chapter 4
The Ego Has Landed

'Most people are other people. Their
thoughts are someone else's opinions, their
lives a mimicry, their passions a quotation.'
Oscar Wilde

IN THE FIRST MONTHS OF LIFE babies scrutinize
their hands intently. Using their fledgling skills of
coordination they are often seen just about managing
to lift a few digits into view for a couple of minutes of
intense observation. After that they might thrust them
into the mouth to study that experience too. Babies are
constantly experimenting. In those first days they don't
know where they begin or where they end. They don't
know who they are or even what a 'who' is. Concepts of
space, time, happiness, sadness, self and non-self do not
exist, indeed they are entirely unfamiliar with anything
we call a concept. They have no language so they have
no thought. What they do have, however, is a rapidly
evolving brain of approximately ten billion buzzing
neurons, hungry to form connections with each other
in a variety of permutations. As learning occurs under
the constant prompting and influence of the adults and
carers around them, these neurons start connecting

away, forming what are known as synapses – junctions – with one another, creating a panoply of circuits. In fact, in the first two years of life a baby forges some 1.8 million synapses a second.

Then, a couple of years later, over fifty percent of these connections are severed through a process of either programmed neuronal death or what is known as 'synaptic pruning' where individual synapses themselves are destroyed. It's a kind of systematic slaughter. Such a mass culling performs a kind of sculpting function, whereby out of the myriad neural connections that a baby formed in those first months of life, only half will ultimately remain. What is left forms their reality. It is these remaining connections that determine how the baby sees the world, feels it, hears it, touches it and tastes it and it is these connections that then go on to determine how that information is processed and interpreted to construct a version of the real world. This will include how they relate to the world as a separate person with notions of 'I' and 'you', 'here' and 'there', all of which will have been taught and repeatedly reinforced by the people around them.

Because every one of us went through this process and, as a result, came out the other end with a concrete sense of self – as distinct from others – we might think that this outcome was inevitable and that the reality each of us now agrees upon is an objective one. But the truth is that this is a reality that was learned and fashioned through that process. It is inevitably a kind of reproduction of the reality fed to us by those already living. And that is what ultimately influenced which circuits in our brain were allowed to remain and which ones would be culled. Indeed the shape and function of our brains are so heavily influenced by those of our parents that studies have shown – at the University of Arizona, for example – that the electroencephalogram (EEG) of a baby mirrors that of the mother so strongly that they peak and trough at the same time whenever they are together. In other words, the function of the baby's brain, as measured in the EEG, is acting as a kind of miniature replica of the mother's. The baby's experience of the world, therefore, cannot be other than that of the mother's, and this will ultimately influence which cells stay and which cells go as the brain takes shape. Doubtless some of the cell death is genetically programmed too, but that is also just another way in which our ancestors' own interpretation of reality came to influence ours. For each circuit that survives the culling period, an equal number perish and, with them, alternative ways of experiencing, sensing and knowing the world.

In this seminal period, therefore, not only are we developing our own brains but, in a very real sense, we are developing our own reality too. This notion has actually been proven experimentally in other animals. For example, in a famous 1974 experiment, a series of cats were raised in an environment where they only ever saw vertical lines. Then, some time later, a horizontal bar was introduced into the cage and the cats walked straight into it, entirely unable to perceive the object. Up to that point, vertical demarcation was all they knew and so, to them, the horizontal form simply did not exist.

The way in which our sense of reality is moulded by the community and experience around us is articulated in typically insightful fashion by psychologist Steven Hayes, Foundation Professor at the University of Nevada:

> First, words such as 'here' and 'there' are acquired which do not apply to a specific thing but to a relation to the child's point of view. For example, 'there' is always anywhere but 'here', and 'here is always 'from this locus or point of view.' Second, children are taught to distinguish their perspective from that of others. Young children have a hard time with the issue of perspective. For example, young children sitting across from a doll will, when asked, report that the doll sees what they are seeing. Gradually, however, a sense of perspective emerges. A child learns what he or she sees is seen from a perspective. Similarly, a young child asked what she had for breakfast, may respond with what her brother ate, but an older child will not make such a mistake. Through correction ('No, that is what your brother ate. What did you eat?') a child must learn to see things from a consistent locus.

This way, the sense that 'I am here', and 'You are there' becomes increasingly concrete. And as we grow older, this sense of being an 'I' that is 'here' looking out upon a world out 'there' continues to evolve in complexity, with layer after layer of detail heaped upon the notion of 'I'. These include likes and dislikes, tastes and traits, beliefs and convictions and all manner of personality facets that make us feel individual. And as this happens, an ever-winding narrative evolves, telling us the story of who we are and what we're like.

This story is our ego. It is a construct of the brain, which is itself a product of the environment in which it was conceived and raised.

In Acceptance and Commitment Therapy (ACT), this aspect of ourselves is known as the conceptualized self, and it is described by the Australian physician and psychotherapist, Russ Harris, in his book *ACT Made Simple*, as follows:

> The conceptualized self (is) all the beliefs, thoughts, ideas, facts, images, judgements, memories, and so on, that form my self concept, that describe 'who I am' as a person: my self description.

This device that our brain uses becomes so solid that it ends up being integral to its very way of working. Ultimately, all actions become interpreted as actions done by the 'I'. So 'chewing' becomes 'I chew', 'walking' becomes 'I walk', and so forth. Indeed, our very notion of existence becomes wrapped up in the 'I'. So that simply 'being' becomes 'I am'.

The ego is essentially an idea – a perspective – generated by our brain, but it is the most pervasive and powerful idea of all. Indeed, it becomes the very focus of all our inner machinations and it starts to exert a gravitational force around itself. A vicious cycle of thought thus emerges, as our brain descends into an endless whirl of chatter. Through the 'I' it can now pontificate, judge, assess, reminisce, analyse, project, plan and ruminate every minute of our waking lives. And because it becomes so dependent – literally addicted – to the ego idea, it must constantly continue to prove and justify its existence as the centre of the only reality it now perceives. The resources of our brain are thus dedicated to maintaining it, with a never-ending firing of neural circuitry fuelling the constant chatter. And that is how most of us exist, trapped in a cyclone of complexity and clutter, because the bottom line is all about the 'I'.

The brain is so invested in the 'I' that the very language we develop is centred around it. You will note while reading this that there is no way that I can write about the 'I' without using phrases that implicitly validate its existence – even in this very sentence, for example, 'you will note' and 'I can write'. The notion of the 'I' – the ego – is the primary lens through which our entire perspective on reality is filtered, from the way we communicate to the way we think.

The term ego, of course, was first coined by Sigmund Freud. He too used it, in some respect, as a means of conceptualizing our individual sense of personality. And by delving deep into it, he helped us understand just how much work we are having to do to maintain the ego all the time. The ego, he said, is in constant compromise between two fundamental and opposing forces that define our life experience: the id and the superego. The id essentially comprises our instinctual drives that are biologically determined, and the superego is an opposing force that centres around conscience, social awareness and guilt. Our sense of self is constantly buttressed by both these forces, as we endlessly try to figure out who exactly we are. And so we are locked in an almost futile struggle to define a stable sense of self. Conclusions shift constantly like a ship on stormy seas. Today I am this, tomorrow I am that. Today I like this, tomorrow I like that.

Freud's descriptions, I believe, were extremely valuable in helping us to understand the perpetual strain that our notion of ego is under. Add to this our constantly changing bodies and drives, and the ever-evolving societal roles we are faced with throughout life, and it's no wonder that our ego requires so much energy to maintain. This is why Freud also acknowledged that this sense of self we concoct is indeed, basically, an unstable entity. 'The ego is not master in its own house,' he wrote.

The ego's primary characteristic is the sense of separation that such an identity creates. And the inevitable consequence of this is judgement. That from which we feel separated is experienced as 'the other'. And so, in seeing the world through our egos, we see a world of separates. The only perception we understand is one in which everything is separated out from everything else. This is basically how logic works. We attempt to study the world around us by dividing it into small pieces. It's the only system we've been brought up to use to make sense of things, and this thought-based conceptual logical framework essentially characterizes the modern world. Each perception is defined by contrasting it to something else, and everything is analysed by breaking it down into smaller and smaller separated chunks.

So July is described as separate from August, night is defined a distinct from day, morning is conceptualized as separate from afternoon and on it goes. We do it with everything we perceive: the tree is conceptualized as other than the field, and the life-form living in the tree is conceptualized as other than the tree. We may accept, on one level, that all of these distinctions are possibly arbitrary, but because we have been schooled in our ego-based separation perspective, since those earliest months of life, the genuine interconnectedness of all these things is not a reality we can fundamentally appreciate.

It is as if, in creating ego, our brains ended up creating a Frankenstein's monster that has removed us from the reality we reside in. The only way we feel we can know something is by labelling it and, in so doing, giving it a separate identity in its own right. Language – the most basic tool and consequence of ego – is all about labelling. And, over time, the label itself conjures up its own reaction, which then removes us by one step from the object or experience that the label describes. So not only is language separating things out, it also performs the function of putting a cloud of associated feelings and concepts around everything we encounter. We know this because words trigger off all sorts of responses within us, even when they are used in purely abstract form, for example just words on a piece of paper. Consider the following:

On the floor behind you is a pool of writhing snakes; a mass of oily skin glinting in the light, with the occasional tongue furtively darting out, eyes that burn with growing hunger, and a constant hiss that seems to pierce your very ear drums with its sharpness.

In most cases, some of the reaction you would have had to the real thing will have been triggered within you by the words on the page alone. This shows how, on some level, we're emotionally prone to reacting to these representations of reality as if they were forms of reality themselves. This is how the mere act of using language takes us away from experiencing the world, on some level, as it really is.

Fundamentally, labelling something is always a way of relating it to something else. If we call something X, then we are saying that it automatically is not Y. This then means that we can start comparing X to Y in all manner of ways: maybe X is heavier than Y, maybe it is hotter, faster, louder, more expensive, more glamorous, less expensive, more important, and the list goes on. So we enter into a world where things are analysed, estimated and valued in their automatic – sometimes unspoken – relationship with other things. Nothing can be experienced for what it is; it is always experienced in conjunction with the labels placed upon it and all the emotions and relativistic comparisons that this then triggers. Through language and logic our ego, therefore, manages basically to keep us lost in our heads.

All this, of course, has its valid uses. It is what makes us such a creative and innovative species, but the problem is that, for most of us, it is also something that we can't control. As described in the previous chapters, the mere act of observing your thoughts will impress upon you that they are not under your constant control. Yet many of us remain embedded in the notion that this constant cloud of thoughts is who we really are – it is the core construct of our identity. It is this tendency to fuse with our thoughts that makes us prone to emotional disturbance, psychological turmoil and mental illness, in a way that is unique to our species. As our sense of ego constantly gyrates, it drags us into cycles of happiness and sadness, positivity and negativity, hope and despair, and everything in between. It's a self-perpetuating merry-go round; a compulsive cycle, that leaves us feeling like we're teetering on the edge of mental breakdown half of the time. That's why so many people are secretly afraid of becoming mentally ill, because the vulnerability is actually very real. This is what creates the dark side of the human condition.

An illustration of this is the fact that there is no consistent record of any species, other than humans, experiencing mental anguish to the point of deliberately and voluntarily taking their own lives.

So ego is an inherently unstable structure, yet it is what we base our lives upon. It represents who we think we are, and it constructs the binoculars through which we view the world – binoculars that become so intoxicating that we fuse them to our eyes, and buy into the notion that there is no way to experience reality other than through them.

The two fundamental aspects of ego are language and logic. But the irony is that, though logic may be the child of ego, its conclusions are frequently capable of disproving its very existence. There are, indeed, a variety of methods through which logic can disprove the validity of ego. In fact, science bumps up against this all the time. Using logic in any direction will ultimately demonstrate that the idea of a separate self is actually wholly illusory, and in the next chapter we will explore a few examples that illustrate just this.

Chapter 5

The Separation Illusion

'Our separation from each other is an optical illusion of consciousness.'

Albert Einstein

WHAT WE CALL EGO is the perspective that we are individual separate entities. It is based on the notion that the 'I' we think we are is a solid, definable, discrete person who is delineated by our body. We tend to see our boundary as our skin – this is the dividing line between 'me' and 'not me'. Yet, in infancy this 'me' existed in a much smaller body, surrounded by a much smaller coat of skin, and if someone asks you, looking at a photograph of that time, 'Was that you?' you'd say 'Yes.' When we went to school, we were still the same 'me', only our boundary was very different again, and in adulthood it changed yet further. Indeed, it changes all the time as we gain and lose weight, age and change shape. And if something dramatic happens, like a limb being amputated, or maybe two, I shall still be the same 'I' I was before the procedure. All in all, the boundary between ourselves and the rest of the world is not very consistent.

When we look at the way we speak, the notion becomes even cloudier. When we talk about 'my legs', 'my arms', 'my body', 'my head', we are talking from the perspective that there is an independent 'me' that is not any of these things. My legs, arms, body and so on are all possessions of 'mine' – a deeper 'me' than all of this. Where the limits of this 'me' lie is, therefore, not strictly definable. We are talking about being an entity without specific edges. Professor Steven Hayes points out that this takes us fairly rapidly to a stark conclusion: 'The only events which are without edges are nothing and everything. Experientially, we are everything/nothing.'

But, because of a combination of our conditioning and inheritance, as outlined in the previous chapter, we don't feel like this most of the time. The extent to which this ego-based perspective of ours is a narrow and skewed version of reality, however, becomes even more obvious when we take a closer look at what our bodies actually are. Our physical bodies are composed of a series of elements. Carbon is the most important, but there are dozens of others like hydrogen, oxygen, calcium, sodium, potassium, chlorine and many more. Each of these elements is subject to something known as a nutrient cycle; this describes how each nutrient moves from the physical environment into living organisms and ultimately back into the physical environment again. This movement is essential for the survival of all of life – plants, animals and the entire ecosystem.

If we look at the nutrient cycle of carbon, for example, we see that carbon is present in large quantities in the air in the form of carbon dioxide. Plants then take this carbon dioxide from the air and, through photosynthesis, convert it to carbon-based molecules of sugar, starch, protein and other foods. It is then consumed in this form by animals, meaning the carbon has now passed from the air to plant life to animal life. The carbon then gets passed along the food chain until it might end up being consumed by humans. This carbon is the essential component of pretty much all biological molecules, and virtually every part of our bodies is made up of molecules that contain carbon. Our blood cells are made of carbon, cells in our gut are made of carbon, our liver cells are made of carbon, the bone in our skeleton is made of carbon; you name it, it's built out of carbon-based molecules. But once they're inside our bodies, they don't just sit there like bricks in a house. In fact, in no sense are our bodies permanent structures. They are actually in a constant process of renewal and re-creation, a perpetual flux.

The cells in the lining of our stomach, for example, last only 5 days. Our red blood cells last about 4 months, and our liver has a turnover time of about 12–18 months. Indeed, our entire skeleton is thought to be replaced about once every 10 years, and the whole of our skin is replaced about once a month. In fact, throughout life, 500,000 cells die every second, 30 million every minute and 50 billion every day. That's why we have so much to excrete. The average person produces about 500 litres of urine a year, as well as over 200 litres of sweat and 300 litres of saliva. We also produce about 150 kilograms of faeces a year too. And our skin is a major source of excretion as well; we shed at least 600,000 particles of skin an hour, which makes up about 80% of the dust in our homes.

All this fluid, dust and solid matter will usually find its way back into the soil. There it is broken down by fungi and bacteria, releasing individual carbon atoms back into the air as carbon dioxide. And here the whole cycle starts again.

The carbon cycle is, of course, just one of over a dozen cycles that are going on all the time for each of the nutrients that make up our bodies, and these cycles are also constantly intersecting with one another. In the oxygen cycle, for example, the carbon dioxide in the air is, as we know, being absorbed by plants. Photosynthesis converts some of this to starch and sugars – as part of the carbon cycle, described above – but the conversion of the carbon dioxide also produces oxygen. This oxygen is discharged into the air, which is then breathed in by us. We use the oxygen to break down carbohydrates in our bodies to produce energy. This process generates more carbon dioxide, which is then, in turn, exhaled back into the atmosphere. We can see, therefore, just how closely intermingled the oxygen and carbon cycles are.

So oxygen, just like carbon, and nitrogen and sodium and all the other elements that we are made out of, is constantly shifting from being part of us, to part of a plant, to part of the atmosphere, to part of an animal, in all sorts of permutations, all the time. In other words, much of what I call 'me' today will be 'you' tomorrow, and what will be 'you' tomorrow will be in the air after that, and a large part of what I call 'a plant' next week will be 'me' soon after that, and so on. We're not just dependent on one another in many respects, we actually *are* one another. And this sense of enmeshed existence is evident at every level. The notion of a separate anything is a tenuous one on all scales.

Let's look at the level of the cell. These are said to be the discrete individual building blocks that are fundamental to every form of life. Each cell is supposed to be seen as a separate unit. But a closer look shows this to be an equally weak proposition. A bit like us, the cell has a kind of skin, called the membrane, which is described as the dividing line between its inside and its outside. This boundary is actually a layer of lipids (organic fats). This means that anything that is soluble in lipid compounds can pass easily across this barrier – that includes oxygen, carbon dioxide and alcohol among others. What can't pass through this layer of lipids, however, are substances that are not soluble in lipids, but are soluble in water instead. But even these can find ways right through the cell membrane, because the lipid layer itself is punctuated by proteins. Many of these proteins are curled up to form channels through which water-soluble substances like sodium, potassium and glucose, for example, can pass freely. So the composition of the inside of a cell is constantly mixing with whatever is floating around outside it. In fact the contrast between the inside and the outside of a cell – in terms of ingredients – is often no more than the contrast between one end of a cell and the other. The cell, therefore, is neither a constant nor a consistent entity; it is forever in flux – just like us. The idea of a static individual, whether at the cellular level or the organism level, is thus not really sustainable. There is no constant 'me', just as there is no single cell that is a constant entity either.

Yet, being a constant person is exactly how we see ourselves. We tell ourselves all the time, 'This is the real me,' or 'This is who I am.' But there is no constant 'this' to speak of. Not even for a single one of our cells.

This lack of consistency at every level leads us to question the very concept of life itself – at least, the notion of separately existing forms of life. The physicist David Bohm, from whom we will hear more later, asks the pointed question, 'At which point can we say that there is a sharp distinction between what is alive and what is not?' So, far from finding any answers, asking the question 'What is me, and what is not me?' only throws up the deeper question of 'What is alive and what is dead?'

Bohm then takes this logic to its ultimate conclusion. He observes that a molecule of carbon dioxide 'that crosses a cell boundary into a leaf does not suddenly "come alive" nor does a molecule of oxygen suddenly "die" when it is released into the atmosphere. Rather, life itself has to be regarded as belonging in some sense to a totality, including plant and environment.'

It appears, therefore, that the question 'Where do I start and where do I end?' is an almost impenetrable one.

Indeed, if we take this quest to a deeper level still – the atomic and subatomic realm – then we see that, even on a temporary basis, the notion of anything existing as a separate entity is, in fact, wholly illusory. At the very smallest and most fundamental level of space and time – particle by particle and moment by moment – the very concept of separation in any shape or form becomes completely untenable. Not only are the lines of division between things constantly in flux, there is actually no demonstrable division at all. As the US physicist, Fritjof Capra put it,

> Quantum theory . . . reveals an essential inter-connectedness of the universe. It shows that we cannot decompose the world into independently existing smallest units . . . The basic oneness of the universe is not only the central characteristic of mystical experience, but is also one of the most important revelations of modern physics.

To understand this properly, we need to get into a little history of particle physics, starting with the idea of the atom, which goes back thousands of years. Before anyone ever observed any such thing, Aristotle posited that there must be an 'uncuttable', irreducible, indestructible form of matter that lies at the base of everything that exists. These were the building blocks of matter, he believed, and, indeed, as science and mathe-matics progressed the concept of the atom became increasingly accepted. Two thousand years later, one of the godfathers of modern physics, Isaac Newton, described what he believed were 'solid, massy, hard, impenetrable, movable particles . . . and that these primitive particles being solids, are incomparably harder than any porous bodies compounded of them; even so very hard as to never wear or break in pieces.'

In 1909, however, a physicist by the name of Ernest Rutherford took the first step in proving that the world at the level of the atom was, in fact, a whole lot weirder than anyone had imagined. In his famous gold foil experiment, he fired radioactive particles at minutely thin strips of gold foil. He then erected screens on the other side of the foil that would be able to detect whether or not any of the radioactive particles were getting through and, if so, where they were landing. What he discovered was that seven out of eight of these particles were actually flying straight through the gold foil, and only one in eight was being deflected. In other words, most of the gold before him was, in fact, empty space. From this he deduced his model of the atom, which suggested that most of the mass of the atom was contained in a small positively charged nucleus at the centre, and the rest of it was empty space, with only a few negatively charged electrons orbiting round the nucleus.

A couple of decades later, however, even this model became obsolete. When physicists started to experiment with matter at the subatomic level, they found themselves forced to throw all their pre-conceived notions of reality out of the window. As the Nobel Prize-winning physicist Eugene Wigner wrote on quantum physics back in 1969, 'The ordinary laws of physics and chemistry' as they had previously been known, 'are a matter of the past.'

In formulating the laws of quantum physics (or quantum mechanics, as it is otherwise known) – looking at matter even smaller than the level of the atom – physicists had to go back to the drawing board to wholly reappraise their understanding of reality. What was known before was referred to as 'classical physics', and they found that every phenomenon that could be described and explained with the laws of classical physics – from the mechanics of an airplane to the motion of the planets – could also be explained equally well using the wholly different laws of quantum physics. But, in addition to this, many phenomena that classical physics failed to explain, like the physics of the newborn universe, or the way that stars burn, could be accurately explained and predicted through the laws of quantum physics. Indeed, not a single one of the theory's predictions has ever been proved wrong. As a result, quantum physics has been responsible for an entire wave of new technologies that we now use all the time, such as lasers, transistors, semiconductors, PET scans and MRI machines. In fact, one third of our economy involves products designed with it.

As Vlatko Vedral, Professor of Physics at Oxford University, put it recently, 'Rarely was a revolution so absolute. Within a decade or so the cast iron laws that underpinned physics since Newton's day were swept away. Classical certainty ceded its stewardship of reality to the probabilistic rule of quantum mechanics.'

The problem, however, is that the laws of quantum mechanics themselves represent a reality so radically different from anything science has ever conceived that many physicists prefer not to think about it. Those who do, however, aren't shy about professing just how dumbstruck the whole thing leaves them. As the famous physicist Niels Bohr – one of the original pioneers of quantum physics – put it, 'Anyone not yet shocked by quantum mechanics has not yet understood it.'

Another renowned physicist, Michio Kaku, summarized the paradox succinctly, 'It is often stated that of all the theories proposed in this century, the silliest is quantum theory. In fact, some say that the only thing quantum theory has going for it is that it is unquestionably correct.' And the physicists Bruce Rosenblum and Fred Kuttner, in their book *Quantum Enigma*, put it this way: 'The worldview demanded by quantum theory is not only stranger than we might suppose, it's stranger than we can suppose.'

The basic findings and theories of quantum physics stem from a single experiment, known as the double-slit experiment that was first conducted way back in 1801 by English polymath Thomas Young. At the time there was a debate going on as to whether or not light was made of a series of individual particles (which we now call photons) or actual waves. His idea was to shine light through a black curtain with two vertical slits and then put a card on the other side to observe how the light landed. He started the experiment with a single slit open only. When he shone the beam of light at it, the card showed a rough line directly opposite the slit composed of a series of dots, as one would expect from particles.

He then went on to pass the beam of light through twin slits. Given the previous result, one would expect, this time, a simple image on the card of two lines, opposite the slits, around which the photons had coalesced. After all, this is how single particles would behave. But that wasn't what he found at all. Instead he saw a series of alternating dark and light bands on the card, as if he was looking at zebra stripes. Particles wouldn't behave that way at all. But he knew something else that would: waves.

If you imagine a sink full of water, and you splash it a little bit at each end, you will create two part-circles of rippling waves that are headed towards each other and towards the edges of the sink. At some point the waves will merge with one another. When that happens we will see them reinforce each other – the peaks become twice as high and the troughs become twice as low. This is called an interference pattern. Imagine that the water is dyed red and we place a sheet of paper on one side of the sink, just facing the area where the waves are merging. When the waves of this interference pattern hit the sheet and stain it, we will see a series of darker and lighter bands where the interference waves hit – a bit like what Young saw on his card. In other words, it is waves that normally produce this kind of alternating dark and light interference pattern when they are set off next to one another and start to merge in this way.

So if light is actually a series of waves, then Young's interference pattern is what you would expect. The initial stream of waves would spread out and then travel through the twin slits. Ripples would emerge from each slit, and they would interfere with one another, creating exactly the interference pattern he observed. This is how an initial single stream of waves, when travelling through two slits, ultimately interferes with itself. Waves can do that, but particles can't. Only, what Young saw wasn't exactly what you'd expect from pure waves either, because he could also see that each dark band contained lots of dots, as if they were particles that hit the screen. This didn't make any sense. If they were individual particles then they would clearly have formed two relatively distinct lines, rather than a series of lines. Particles are distinct. A particle can't interfere with itself to create such bands, yet somehow it looked like that was exactly what was happening.

So, was light made up of waves or particles? The only answer Young could provide was that it must be both. But this was not in any way logically consistent. By definition a particle is a single discrete boundaried entity, and a wave is almost exactly the opposite – smeared out and interconnected with all its surroundings. Yet the light seemed to be behaving as if it were both of these entirely contradictory things.

People tried to ignore these nonsensical findings for many years, in the hope that it was just some quirky property of light that we couldn't quite understand. But then the same experiment was performed with electrons – the stuff of solid matter – and they behaved in exactly the same way too.

Each electron was observed through an electron microscope leaving the source and then, after passing through one of the two slits, landing on a detector plate. But, after enough were fired, they seemed somehow to line up in an interference pattern. Again, it was as if each electron was in two places at once, interfering with itself. But how could an electron be in two places at once?

To try and resolve this unfathomable paradox, physicists decided next to place a measuring device next to the slits so that they could observe which slit the electron was passing through or if indeed it was somehow in two places at once. The experiment was run again and the scientists in the lab sat back and watched.

This time they were looking right at the centre of action. What was actually occurring here?

The particles were observed to be behaving as one might have conventionally expected, namely; each electron passed through either one of the slits – one at a time. But then, when they looked across at the detector screen where the particles were landing, this time they noticed that the interference pattern had disappeared – it contained just two lines of particles, one opposite each slit, just as you would expect from pure particles, not waves. The mere act of observing the electrons passing through the slits led to the interference pattern disappearing and the individual electrons acting like individual particles again. When the measuring devices by the slits were removed, then, lo and behold, the interference pattern returned. In other words, when the particles were observed in action, they behaved as particles and when they were left alone, they behaved more like waves. The observation itself seemed profoundly to affect the reality being observed.

These experiments have since been performed countless times by numerous scientists over many years, and each time the results have been identical, so much so, that this mind-boggling state of affairs is now beyond dispute. When particles are directly scrutinized for the length of their journey, they look and behave exactly like individual particles. But when left to their own devices and measured at the end of their journey, each particle behaves like a wave and starts interfering with itself. And its not just subatomic particles this has been observed in. The same results have also been found with larger particles, made of several atoms. In other words, the same phenomenon is now being observed in the macro world – way beyond just the quantum, subatomic level – and it has been termed *the observer effect*.

One of the earliest and most commonly cited interpretations of this seemingly inexplicable data is called the Copenhagen Interpretation. It was derived by Nobel Prize-winning physicists Werner Heisenberg and Niels Bohr, together with Erwin Schrödinger and several notable others who worked together in Copenhagen in the late 1920s, and it remains – for the majority of scientists – the most convincing explanation and mathematical description of these phenomena to date. But it is no less revolutionary or breath-taking for that. They do not deny that a mere act of observation can alter reality; indeed, they base their theory upon this evidently unchallengeable fact.

The Copenhagen Interpretation suggests that, before it is observed, matter exists in the form of potential only: a kind of wave of probability. This state of affairs is called a quantum superposition. The electron, for example, exists in many places at the same time, but nowhere specifically has it actually manifested. They devised an equation that describes how matter exists in this form of wave, a kind of half state – not there, but not 'not there' either – and this was called Schrödinger's wave equation. And it only manifests in the form of actual tangible matter when it is observed. This is called a quantum collapse, or collapsing the wave function. Up until the observation, matter is just a cloud of possibility, smeared out across a broad area. Indeed, the equations they produced enabled them to draw what are known as probability density clouds, which are three-dimensional zones in which the electrons have a probability of manifesting as solid particles *if* observed there. But even those aren't definitive, for, according to the maths, any electron can technically pop up if observed anywhere. It's just more likely to do so in certain areas.

Physicists Bruce Rosenblum and Fred Kuttner describe its implications in *Quantum Enigma*: 'If someone looked in a particular spot and happened to see the atom there, that look "collapsed" the spread out waviness of that atom to be wholly at that particular spot . . . According to quantum theory, there was not an actual atom in a particular place before we looked.'

Werner Heisenberg was unambiguous about its meaning too, 'The atoms or elementary particles themselves are not real; they form a world of potentialities or possibilities rather than one of things or facts.'

Such notions are of course startling to anyone who encounters them, just as they were to the founders of the theory themselves, and just about every eminent physicist around the world ever since. The renowned French theoretical physicist Bernard d'Espagnat put it like this, 'The doctrine that the world is made up of objects whose existence is independent of human consciousness turns out to be in conflict with quantum mechanics and with facts established by experiment.' And the prolific American theoretical physicist Fred Wolf, surmised that, 'The observer effect says that there is no reality until that reality is perceived. This profound insight tells us that we alter every object in the world simply by paying attention to it.'

So here we learn that observation is, in fact, central to the very existence of matter itself. Mind is integral to matter. And the Nobel Prize-winning physicist Eugene Wigner, tells us that, 'It was not possible to formulate the laws of quantum mechanics in a fully consistent way without reference to consciousness.'

As a result, this has got forward-thinking psychiatrists interested too. Professor Jeffrey Schwartz, in his book *The Mind and the Brain*, notices that,

> The role of observation in quantum physics cannot be emphasized too strongly. In classical physics observed systems have an existence independent of the mind that observes and probes them. In quantum physics, however, only through an act of observation does a physical quantity have an actual value.

This is, therefore, not just a theory of matter, it is a theory of mind too, and how the two interact.

The theory goes yet deeper, however, when it explains what happens when two separate unobserved objects interact. According to quantum theory, when two or more particles come together, in their 'uncollapsed' state – when they are just probability clouds, described as wave functions – they become 'entangled'. This means that they continue to behave as if they are still linked to each other, even if they are subsequently miles apart.

Despite being very uneasy about quantum theory, Einstein was the one who predicted this implication of it. He actually predicted it – together with two other colleagues, Podolsky and Rosen – as a thought experiment by which he intended to demonstrate flaws in the theory. Their challenge became known as the EPR Paradox, after its proposers. They deduced that for quantum theory to be right, two particles that were once entangled should ultimately, when separated out and 'collapsed', still be able to affect one another even from great distances apart. To Einstein this was just taking the weirdness of quantum theory too far. He described it as 'spooky action at a distance'.

Unfortunately for Einstein, 28 years after his death, in 1982, once the technology to do it became available, French Physicist, Alain Aspect did an experiment that showed how quantum entanglement had exactly the implications that Einstein predicted. Aspect fired an originally entangled pair of photons in opposite directions and then he affected the spin of one merely by observing it. He then measured the spin of the other one – far away – millionths of a second later, and found that it had an exactly corresponding spin to the first particle. The first one had, then, somehow affected the spin of the second one without being anywhere near it and, indeed, far enough away, for not even light to have passed between the two in the time allowed.

In other words, by observing one of a pair of entangled particles and having an effect on it, by dint of the observation, the other entangled particle was immediately affected, even though it was far away. The experiment was carried out across larger and larger distances and every time the result was the same. Somehow, two particles that were once entangled were behaving as if they were the same unit. This is known in physics as nonlocality, where two entities separated in space and time are able to affect each other without anything passing in between them, therefore acting as if not separated at all.

But, here's the rub. According to the Big Bang theory, we were all entangled once. Every cell, every atom, every electron that makes us up is entangled with every other in the whole universe. Nonlocality should apply to all of us. So it's not just that the atoms that we are composed of are constantly mixing with our environment and the world around us, they actually behave as if they *are* every other atom in the Universe, at the same time.

This is when our ability to conceptualize reality starts to break down. We can no longer rely on logic to comprehend the enormity of what this means because, if everything is so deeply and constantly at one with everything else, then we are calling into question the very notions of space and time we use to navigate our way logically through life.

But then again, perhaps we always knew this.

It seems to me that most of us actually have an appreciation of this fundamental reality, somewhere inside of us, even if it defies our very ability to conceptualize the world we live in. We will often feel, for example, that coincidences that cannot be explained by logic are meaningful to us. We might sense that a seemingly random event actually seems to correlate with something going on in our lives at that very moment, in a way we could not even begin to explain. And though our sceptical mind might try to pooh-pooh the notion as a form of meaningless coincidence, deep down inside we still sense that there is some reality to this.

This notion of our profound interconnectedness is actually an instinct we have never lost. Indeed the experience is so common that the famous psychiatrist Carl Jung wrote a whole book about it, called *Synchronicity*. Jung genuinely believed that there was real meaning behind such events, and it was a particular experience with a patient that launched his investigation into the subject. He was seeing a woman whose dreams he analysed during the course of their therapy sessions. At one point she described a dream involving a very rare insect called a Golden scarab, technically known as *Cetonia aurata*. During the session, Jung heard something tapping on the window behind him. He turned round and opened the window, and in flew a scarabaeid beetle, which he caught in his hand. Its gold-green colour resembled exactly that of the rare *Cetonia aurata* of the woman's dream.

To him and to his patient, this event was far more meaningful than pure coincidence. After that, he started to realize that such synchronicities actually occur in our lives all the time. We just have to open our eyes and still our logical mind to become aware of them. As he put it, 'Synchronicity is an ever present reality for those who have eyes to see.'

Now, fascinatingly, science is telling us that such synchronicities are indeed based on actual reality – a deeper reality than perhaps our logical, ego-focused thinking brain is capable of comprehending. Mathematics and physics have got to a point where such experiences of deep interconnection with all around us can be shown to have a real validity. It's just hard to define it logically and tangibly without the maths and physics as pointers.

One of the original pioneers and deepest thinkers in the realm of quantum physics was David Bohm. In his classic book *Wholeness and the Implicate Order*, he wrote, 'Ultimately the entire universe has to be understood as a single undivided whole, in which analysis into separately and independently existing parts has no fundamental status.'

He subsequently devised an ingenious illustration to explain how this might work at the most basic level of matter. The illustration he provided has in fact become, to many, one of the most powerful metaphors ever created by a physicist to convey the fundamental nature of reality as revealed by quantum mechanics.

It starts with a single fish swimming in a fish tank. Imagine that there are two video cameras pointing towards the fish tank. One camera is pointing at the front wall of the tank, and the other camera is pointing at a side wall of the fish tank. The cameras are, therefore, at ninety degrees to each other. In addition, each camera is also connected to a separate television monitor.

If we now observe the images on each monitor, they appear to be very different. When one monitor shows the head of a fish looking directly at it, the other will show the side of the fish. A casual observer - unaware of the fish tank itself - could easily believe that what she was observing on the screens were different fish. As she continues to observe both monitors, she will notice that every time one fish moves, the other also moves. It almost seems like they are, in some way, communicating with one another – but via some 'spooky' method that appears to travel faster than the speed of light. This, of course, is an exact analogy of how entangled particles seem to affect one another, despite being far apart.

Bohm is suggesting, therefore, that in the same way that the observation of two separate fish is an illusion, so is the observation that there are separate particles. They are merely projections of different aspects of the same underlying reality. Every one of us, every object, every creature, every particle is essentially a projection of a different aspect of the same underlying reality.

The world we see around us, which our brains have trained us to believe is real, is a version of the TV screens Bohm described. This is what produces the illusion of separation. It's a bit like a hologram where the image we see is a form of optical illusion produced by a deeper reality behind it. Bohm commented:

> What should be said is that wholeness is what is real, and that fragmentation is ... guided by illusory perception, which is shaped by fragmentary thought. All our different ways of thinking are to be considered as different ways of looking at the one reality.

This description also explains the observer effect. If we're all projections of the same unity, then you'll always have an effect on something when you're trying to observe it, because you happen also to be the thing you are trying to observe. It becomes like a dog chasing its tail, or perhaps like looking at yourself in the mirror; you always have to move yourself in order to do it.

In this view, then, every single thing in the universe is merely a projection of the one unified reality. In other words, every 'thing' is, in fact, everything. At the same time, this deeper reality is not something we can ever directly see or conceive of through our mind and ordinary senses, as it exists on a different plane of reality altogether. It is not any 'thing' that we can perceive. In other words, it is 'nothing'. Every 'thing' is hence both everything and nothing.

The fact that mainstream science has derived these conclusions is what makes them so unsettling for many of us. And the part of us that is unsettled by them is our ego; this sense of being an individual 'I'. Understandably, our sense of being an individual 'I' will experience considerable discomfort at the realization of such notions. Even if logical reasoning is a product of ego itself, the fact that its ultimate application – science – can point us towards the reality of our true wholeness, will inevitably evoke fear and anxiety within ego. As a result, scientific progress is often met with harsh resistance from within its own ranks.

In 1894, for example, the eminent physicist and Nobel Prize-winner Albert Michelson declared,

> The more important and fundamental laws and facts of physical science have all been discovered, and these are now so firmly established that the possibility of their ever being supplanted in

consequence of new discoveries is exceedingly
remote . . . Future discoveries must be looked for
in the sixth place of decimals.

And several years later, in 1900, the physicist and
inventor Lord Kelvin – William Thomson – supposedly
insisted, 'There is nothing new to be discovered in
physics now. All that remains is more and more precise
measurements.'

All of this was before the revolutions of quantum
physics, relativity, the Big Bang theory and much more –
which have transformed the very nature of science, and,
indeed, its understanding of nature itself. We now sit on
a precipice in which an entirely new understanding of
reality can be used to solve all manner of problems from
the ecological to the economic, and from the sociological
to the psychiatric. Yet, despite this, resistance continues.
Deepak Chopra – the American physician and prolific
writer – has talked extensively about the implications
of quantum mechanics for modern medicine, and he
is sometimes attacked for doing just this by materialist
scientists and self-styled sceptics such as Richard
Dawkins, for whom anything with even the remotest
spiritual connotation is unacceptable.

The sceptics' argument is that quantum physics is
an entirely separate discipline to medicine and so the
two should not be mixed. The notion that one branch
of science should not be used to inform another is,
of course, never tenable. Without the application of
mathematics and classical physics, we would know
virtually nothing of human physiology or pathology.

What the sceptics are really saying is that they want to draw the line at quantum physics because it challenges their existing world view too much. It's just too uncomfortable for the ego. The safe, separation-based perspective of the world cannot be abandoned. Psychologically, there's just too much invested in it. As a result, attempts to halt such scientific and societal integration continue unabated, as if none of these discoveries had ever been made. In 1997, for example, John Horgan, a senior writer for *Scientific American*, published a book called *The End of Science*. In it he wrote, 'If one believes in science, one must accept the possibility – even the probability – that the great era of scientific discovery is over . . . Further research may yield no more great revelations or revolutions, but only incremental, diminishing returns.'

Yet, in reality, quantum physics and related disciplines have opened the door to a new paradigm – one that we somehow always knew, but never really saw. The separated reality that our senses show us, and that our brains interpret for us is fundamentally an illusion. As the physicist Fred Wolf puts it,

> Distinctions are not real. They are fleeting whispers of an all-pervading, subtle, non-expressive potential reality. The world is not made of separate things. Mind is not separate from matter. And you are not separate from any other being, animal, vegetable, living, dead, or seemingly inanimate matter . . . The greatest illusion of all? The illusion of 'I'. This ever-present I-ness.

Neuroscience is one of the areas in which this battle is being most keenly waged, being central to the arguments over who we are and what the function of our brain really is. Proponents of the reductionist ego paradigm – often referred to as the materialist worldview – are aggressively resisting any talk of paradigm shift and a good overview of the current state of play is depicted within the book *Brain Wars* by eminent neuroscientist Mario Beauregard. In it he points out,

> Physicists were forced to abandon the assumptions of classical physics and the scientific materialist worldview nearly a decade ago, but [these] battles . . . are still being fought by many neuroscientists. The time has come for my colleagues to embrace the many possibilities of the universe opened by the new physics.

The reason, I believe, physicists have been more open to an exploration of levels of reality beyond the layer of separation we normally think we exist in, is that for them this is a relatively abstract investigation. It is about the mathematics of matter and the dry physical theories that flow from it, whereas, when it comes to biology we are getting closer to home. In this field we have to start considering how all of this applies to us personally. This is the point at which the new reality meets the resistance of the ego. This is also why most quantum physicists don't usually spend time contemplating what their findings mean for the nature of consciousness and, indeed, reality itself. The prolific quantum physicist and philosopher Henry Stapp is recorded to have said of his own field, 'Quantum physics is taught as engineering. This is how you apply it and these are the mathematical rules. The philosophy is brushed under the rug. You don't try to think what's really happening.' And the neuropsychiatrist Jeffrey Schwartz, who spent time with some notable physicists during his years of research into consciousness and mental illness, observed,

> For every hundred scientists who use quantum mechanics, applying the standard equations like recipes, probably no more than one ponders the philosophy of it. They don't have to. You can do perfectly good physics if you just 'shut up and calculate,' as the physicist Max Tegmark put it.

A few physicists do, however, think more globally and deeply about their own subject matter. And none of those who do can avoid arriving at the most far-reaching conclusions about the nature of existence. Indeed, many have gone as far as to realize the profound parallels between their work and descriptions of much older times. It was Robert Oppenheimer, father of the atomic bomb, who said,

> The generous notions about human under-standing . . . which are illustrated by discoveries in atomic physics are not in the nature of things wholly unfamiliar, wholly unheard of, or new. Even in our own culture they have a history, and in Buddhist and Hindu thought a more con-siderable and central place.

And in his book *The Tao of Physics*, Fritjof Capra notes that quantum physics does not see the world as a series of independently existing entities, but 'as a complicated web of relations between the various parts of the unified whole'. He then goes on to observe that, 'This, however, is the way in which Eastern mystics have experienced the world, and some of them have expressed their experience in words which are almost identical with those used in atomic physics.'

For, thousands of years before the earth-shattering discoveries of quantum mechanics and the like, there was something within man that spoke to this deeper reality. In some shape or form, spiritual traditions throughout history have been pointing to this fundamental reality since their inceptions. Though, in recent times, Western culture has retreated from religion – often based on valid reasons and concerns – today it risks throwing the baby out with the bathwater, as we discover that logic and science struggle to describe a reality that spiritual wisdom has been pointing to for millennia. And it is to this stream of the human experience that we shall turn in the next chapter.

Chapter 6
The Stream of Spirit

'Faith is not knowledge of what the mystery of
the universe is, but the conviction that there
is a mystery and that it is greater than us.'

Rabbi David Wolpe

HISTORIANS BELIEVE THAT evidence of religion can be
traced as far back as the invention of writing itself, over
5,000 years ago. It appears that when man learned to
write, and thus record his ideas in some form, a sense
of a divine dimension to life was already clearly in
existence. Indeed, before it was ever explicitly written
about, there is evidence that spiritual beliefs and
rituals were an integral part of human custom for many
millennia. Burial rites were being observed within
societies as far back as 25,000 years ago, and the oldest
man-made religious structure – Göbekli Tepe, in Turkey
– is believed to have been constructed over 12,000 years
ago. A spiritual inclination appears to be a fundamental
aspect of the human condition, and today we have a series
of permutations of religious beliefs that are followed by
billions of people around the world. Indeed, over 85%
of the world's population are currently affiliated to a
specific religious faith.

When we consider what we mean by faith, then our definition has to begin with an appreciation that there are aspects of our world that cannot be wholly penetrated by logic alone. To have faith means that there is a form of knowledge that, though it can't be proved, can still be known. Now, in modern times, since the age of the Enlightenment, the notion of knowing anything that can't be explicitly proved has been increasingly dismissed. This is often with good reason too, for faith can lead us down all sorts of blind alleys, as it has throughout history, sometimes causing genuine hardship and damage. But across a variety of traditions today, many are able to guard their spiritual beliefs against the worst aspects of zealotry by maintaining a sense of awe, and an appreciation of the fact that, fundamentally, true faith must necessarily admit doubt. A person of faith who is not a fundamentalist, will be happy to accept that 'This is what I believe,' rather than 'This is what I know.' And the difference between the two is all the difference in the world. A statement of belief is an admission of the subjective nature of the experience. And this exploration of the subjective realm makes spirituality a wholly different path to the scientific one – which is focused more on the objectively verifiable. But given the extent to which the two seem to be meeting, it is becoming increasingly important to look again at the world's faiths as a source of learning, particularly where they intersect.

Among all the myriad scriptures and messages of the world's different religions, a couple of themes seem to be shared. Foremost among these is what has come to be known as the Golden Rule. The Bible incorporates it in various places: 'Love thy neighbour as thyself' (Mark 12: 31), and 'Whatever you wish that men would do to you, do so to them' (Matthew 7: 12). In Islam the same sentiment is written as follows, 'Not one of you is a believer until he loves for his brother what he loves for himself' (*Forty Hadith of an-Nawawi*). And the Jewish Talmud is equally emphatic, 'What is hateful to you, do not to your fellow man. That is the entire Law; all the rest is commentary' (Talmud, *Shabbat* 31a).

Where the more eastern religions are concerned, the Golden Rule is a clear instruction there too. Hindus are told, 'One should not behave towards others in a way which is disagreeable to oneself. This is the essence of morality.' (*Mahabharata*, Anusasana Parva 113: 8). And Buddhism follows suit with, 'Hurt not others in ways that you yourself would find hurtful' (*Udana-Varga* 5: 18). In Taoism the Golden Rule is expressed as, 'Regard your neighbour's gain as your own gain and your neighbour's loss as your own loss' (*T'ai Shang Kan Ying P'ien*), and Zoroastrianism puts it this way, 'That nature alone is good which refrains from doing unto another whatsoever is not good for itself' (*Dadistan-i-dinik* 94: 5).

Virtually every faith carries this same message. It is a message to the whole of creation that no part of it should be considered to be above or below any other. It speaks to a fundamental unity that pervades all, suggesting that, on some fundamental level, both my fellow man and I are one. Indeed, this express notion is laced throughout the texts of every religion, and it appears in a host of different ways. For some faiths, for example, this universal oneness is an explicit attribute of the divine ideal itself, in the form of an omnipresent deity.

Muslims are taught that,

> 'To Allah belongs the east and the west; wherever you go there will be the presence of Allah. Allah is Omnipresent.' (Koran, 2: 115)

And this is echoed in the Bible across a series of passages:

> 'I am the Alpha and the Omega, the first and the last, the beginning and the end.' (Revelation 22: 13)

> 'In Christ were created all things in heaven and on earth; everything visible and everything invisible.' (Colossians 1: 15–17)

> 'One God and Father of all, who is over all and through all and in all.' (Ephesians 4: 6)

> 'And the scribe said to him, "You are right, Teacher. You have truly said that he is one, and there is no other besides him."' (Mark 12: 32)

> 'Where could I go to escape your spirit? Where could I flee from your presence? If I climb the heavens, you are there. There too, if I lie in Sheol. If I flew to the point of sunrise, or westward across the sea your hand would still be guiding me, your right hand holding me.' (Psalm 139: 7–10)

> 'In him we live, and move, and have our being.' (Acts 17: 28)

'For from him, and through him and to him are
all things.' (Romans 8. 36)

Jewish texts are equally peppered with such notions.
The Tanakh, for example, states, 'I am the Lord, and
there is none else. I form the light and create darkness,
I make peace and create evil' (Isaiah, 45: 6–7). And in
the words to a song that Orthodox Jewish children sing
about God (called Hashem in this case), we see: 'Hashem
is here, Hashem is there, Hashem is truly everywhere.
Up, up, down, down, right, left and all around, here,
there and everywhere. That's where he can be found.'

Nothing, of course, can be separate from an omnipresent God. Such a unified nature of being has thus
been spoken of, written down and sung about through
every generation. The reality that modern science has
shone a torch upon was hidden in plain sight along.
And in some scripture passages of the major religions,
this sense of our wholly interconnected union with all
has been cited unambiguously, as in one of the Koran's
core proclamations, 'O mankind! We created you from
a single soul' (49: 13), or the Bible, where it says, 'For in
one Spirit we were all baptized into one body . . . and all
were made to drink of one Spirit' (Corinthians 12: 13).
And 'There is one body and one Spirit' (Ephesians 4: 4).

Of course, we cannot deny that, despite this most
fundamental area of commonality and agreement,
this is not the only perspective contained within conventional religions. Any message of complete unity will
also always represent an existential threat to ego. Even
though ego is essentially no more than an idea – a belief

in a particular perspective – it has obtained such a firm grasp upon our psyche that it leaves us feeling that any threat to it is like a threat to our very existence. Nothing, of course, could be further from the truth, but this is how we feel when our ego-based perspective on life is threatened. This creates backlashes wherever glimpses of our fundamental unity occur. We saw in the last chapter how the scientific journey toward a realization of our deep-seated interconnectedness has faced ego-based resistance throughout history, and continues to be resisted in some quarters to this day, even in the face of such widely established findings. And the spiritual journey is no different: it too is subject to the same ego-driven resistance.

Sometimes ego-based thinking can actively push religions towards a world of concept and logic and, ironically, away from faith. This leads to a conceptualization of the divine that automatically creates a separation between worshippers and the worshipped, for example the perspective of a God on high judging His followers down below. And once the first division has been made, a vicious cycle often sets in – all to quell the anxieties of ego. Anywhere that religion promotes or exacerbates notions of separation is a manifestation of ego, whether that be between God and man, between followers and clergy, or between one faith and another. Such separation is what leads to judgement and judgement is the hallmark of ego. This is how some of the deepest wisdom has in the past, and still in some places today, morphed into the cause of greatest conflict.

In truth, no faith needs to be in conflict with another. They are all *a* path to spiritual wisdom, while none of them is *the* path. Ideas of exclusivity, of being 'the chosen ones' or 'the only way', are sure signs of ego dominance.

Fundamentally, science and spirituality are not in conflict with one another either; it is our ego that is in conflict with both. And just as egocentrism in religion has provoked various attempts to suppress science, so it has led to the suppression of those within religion's own ranks from time to time also.

It is true that throughout the history of religion, there have been groups of people and strands of thought that have held steadfastly to the core common ground of all faiths and promoted unity on all levels: between different faiths, between the worshipper and the worshipped and, indeed, between all of creation. These have often centred around the esoteric branches of particular faiths – the schools of thought that focus on an inner experiential understanding of spirituality, rather than an outer literalist one. In Islam such ideas are referred to as Sufism and in Christianity as Gnosticism. They were driven by an exploration and celebration of this sense of unity and, yet, it is for this very focus and expression that they were sometimes persecuted. Their message, however, remains as inspiring and profoundly resonant today as it has been for hundreds of years.

The story of how the modern world came to under-stand more about Gnosticism is itself a powerful metaphor for just how deeply suppressed its notions had been for much of the last 2,000 years.

It starts with an Egyptian farmer named Muhammad

'Alí al-Sammán. One day in 1945, while travelling to the mountains in search of a form of natural fertilizer known as *sabakh*, he accidentally unearthed a red earthenware jar approximately a metre high in a place called Nag Hammadi. He was reluctant to open it, given all the tales of evil spirits that are commonly associated with buried treasures in that part of the world. He eventually succumbed to the temptation, however, and opened up the jar in search of riches. What he found, however, disappointed him: it was a few dozen books bound in leather cases. Completely oblivious to their value, he returned to his home in a town called al-Qasr and left the books and loose papyrus leaves on the straw piled on the ground next to the oven. His mother then proceeded to burn many of them, using them as fuel for the oven.

After his father's death, Muhammad 'Alí al-Sammán and his brothers became embroiled in a bitter vendetta against the men who they believed were responsible. A bloody feud ensued involving much violence and murder and as, by now, the books were one of Muhammad's few possessions, he left them with a local priest, al-Qummus Basiliyus Abd al-Masih. From there, several of the books found their way onto the Egyptian antiquities market and this brought them to the attention of the Egyptian government, who housed some of them in the Coptic Museum in Cairo. There they remained for a number of years until 1955, when rumours about their existence spread to a Dutch historian, Gilles Quispel. He went to the Coptic Museum in Cairo and was instantly intrigued by what he saw. The texts were scrutinized by several university departments and found to be authentic manuscripts from nearly 2,000 years ago. And they all appeared to be forms of biblical gospel. This was one of the biggest archaeological discoveries in modern times.

Their titles included 'The Gospel of Thomas', 'The Gospel of Mary Magdalene', 'The Gospel of Judas', 'The Gospel of Truth' and many others. Professor Helmut Koester of Harvard University suggested that the collection of sayings in the Gospel of Thomas, for example, although compiled around 140 AD, may include some traditions even older than the gospels of the New Testament, 'possibly as early as the second half of the first century' (50–100 AD).

The idea of a single unified message handed down by the apostles was what much of the official church had propagated for centuries but, as Elaine Pagels, historian, writer and Princeton University Professor of Religion, put it, 'The discoveries at Nag Hammadi have upset this picture. If we admit that some of these fifty-two texts represents early forms of Christian teaching, we may have to recognize that early Christianity is far more diverse than nearly anyone expected before the Nag Hammadi discoveries.'

Indeed, there is evidence, as far back as 180 AD, of powerful figures of the official Roman church, such as Bishop Irenaeus of Lyons, denouncing a series of so called 'heretical' texts for being 'full of blasphemy'. And what was this blasphemy? It was the notion that there is, in fact, no separation between God and man. Pagels discusses how starkly 'Some of the gnostics who wrote these gospels contradict this: self-knowledge is knowledge of God; the self and the divine are identical . . . to know oneself, at the deepest level, is simultaneously to know God; this is the secret of gnosis.'

As the Gnostic teacher, Monoimus puts it:

> Abandon the search for God and the creation and other matters of a similar sort. Look for him by taking yourself as the starting point. Learn who it is within you who makes everything his own and says, 'My God, my mind, my thought, my soul, my body.' Learn the sources of sorrow, joy, love, hate . . . If you carefully investigate these matters you will find him in yourself.

This sentiment runs throughout the Gnostic gospels. Jesus is seen as a guide who is not apart from the rest of humanity, but a pioneer who has achieved full realization of his true nature in a way that is available to all others too. In the Gospel of Thomas, he is quoted as saying, 'I am not your master . . . He who will drink from my mouth will become as I am: I myself shall become he, and the things that are hidden will be revealed to him.' The idea of unity is fundamental to his teaching. At the deepest level of reality, opposites are the same, differences merge, and an underlying oneness prevails:

> Jesus said to them, 'When you make the two into one, and when you make the inner like the outer and the outer like the inner, and the upper like the lower, and when you make male and female into a single one, so that the male will not be male nor the female be female, when you make eyes in place of an eye, a hand in place of a hand,

a foot in place of a foot, an image in place of
an image, then you will enter [the kingdom].'
(Gospel of Thomas, 22)

Today, whether they have heard of Gnosticism or
not, many divisions and churches follow Christianity in
exactly this spirit, and, in my experience, those who gain
most from their religious life, experience and practise it
in this vein too.

All of this resonates profoundly with Sufism in
Islam, which has endured a similar historical fate to
Gnosticism in Christianity. The first Sufi master was
a poet, teacher and dedicated student of the faith by
the name of Hussein Al-Halaj. He was condemned in
922 AD for heresy when, in a state of mystical trance,
he exclaimed, 'I am the Truth.' He was killed and his
remains were burnt in Baghdad.

The persecution of Sufis by the more literalist,
fundamentalist followers of Islam continues to this
day. Hundreds of innocent people have been killed or
wounded in recent waves of attacks on sites considered
sacred to Sufis. On 25 October 2010, for example, an
al-Qaida-affiliated militant group targeted a majestic Sufi
shrine in the Punjab province of Pakistan, detonating
bombs hidden in milk cans and killing and wounding
scores of innocent people.

Whenever the egocentric perspective of the world is
threatened, it bites back. And Sufism was, and still is,
undoubtedly such a threat. Just like the Gnostics before
them, the Sufis celebrate their complete union with the
divine. They talk of an annihilation of the individual ego-

based self in order to facilitate a merging into oneness with God. The Sufi scholar Moulana Shah Maghsoud spoke of knowledge being the ultimate annihilation of the knower into the known. An example of this is a passage narrated by another famous Sufi, Ba Yazid: 'The first time I went on a pilgrimage to Mecca, I saw the House; the second time I saw the Owner of the House; the third time I saw neither the House nor the Owner, for I was annihilated into the Divine.' Attar, another Sufi poet and theoretician, explained how those who are free from ego become united with God. It is at this stage of selflessness that they leave the transient 'self' behind. So annihilation, in this way, becomes the ultimate liberation.

In the book *Principles of Sufism*, contemporary Sufi scholar and human rights activist Nahid Angha points out that,

> Though, through the eyes of matter, there is an apparent boundary around every object, living or inanimate, a boundary that reflects the capacities and uses of the senses, there is no real separation between any real particle of existence. Every element of being is connected and bound to every other.

She, like many millions of Muslims around the world today, practises her religion, not as a pursuit of literal dogma, but as a call to spiritual unity. This profound unity has indeed been a consistent and, often central, theme across different faiths around the globe, and throughout history. Indeed, whenever the ego-dominated factions of any faith have attempted to suppress such expressions, they have always, sooner or later, found a way back.

Some of the earliest articulations of these notions can actually be found in the even more ancient spiritual traditions of the Far East. Around 4,000 years ago, a group of Indo-European people entered the Indian subcontinent through the Hindu Kush mountains. They were known as Aryans. Upon arrival in the Indus River valley, they found a civilization already thousands of years old, and relatively advanced in technology and trade. A key facet of this society were the so called Brahmins, who would serve as priests during ceremonies and rituals but spend most of their time in solitary retreats in the forests. From the fusion of these two cultures Indian civilization was born, and much of its spiritual dimension grew out of the teachings of these forest-dwelling Brahmins. The first written texts of this civilization are known as the Upanishads. 'Upanishad' means 'sitting down near' and it was through such intimate direct sessions that these – the roots of Hinduism – were first conveyed over 2,500 years ago. To the Brahmin, however, they were already considered ancient wisdom, passed orally from one generation to the next, stretching back several thousand years before that.

In his book summarizing the texts, Eknath Easwaran encapsulates their essence beautifully:

> They tell us that there is a Reality underlying life which rituals cannot reach, next to which the things we see and touch in everyday life are shadows. They teach that this Reality is the

essence of every created thing, and the same
Reality is our real Self.

The verses of the Upanishads themselves do not refer
to the divine reality as anything that could be separate
from any part of creation. No name is given to it, but
instead it is referred to in the most intimate way possible
– as the 'Self'.

> The Self is the sun shining in the sky,
> The wind blowing in space; he is the fire
> At the altar and in the home the guest
> He dwells in human beings, in gods, in truth,
> And the vast firmament; he is the fish
> Born in water, the plant growing in the earth,
> The river flowing down from the mountain.
>
> (Katha II)

> He is this boy, he is that girl, he is this man,
> He is that woman, and he is this old man too,
> Tottering on his staff. His face is everywhere.
> He is the blue bird, he is the green bird with
> Red eyes, he is the thundercloud, and he is the
> Seasons and the sea.
>
> (Shvetashvatara IV)

The description, as we can see, is wholly compatible
with the notion of reality that modern science has
unearthed in recent years. All is in one and one is in all:

> There is only one Self in all creatures.
> The One appears many, just as the moon
> Appears many reflected in water.
>
> (Amritabindu XIV)

As by knowing one piece of gold, dear one,
We come to know all things made out of gold.
That they differ only in name and form,
While the stuff of which all are made is gold . . .
So through that spiritual wisdom, dear one,
We come to know that all life is one.

(Chandogya VI)

The texts make a clear distinction between the narrow individually focused perspective of the ego, and that of the infinite oneness that is the Self, and they talk at length about how each of these leads to very different experiences of life:

Two are seated by life's fountain. The separate ego
Drinks of the sweet and bitter stuff,
Liking the sweet, disliking the bitter,
While the supreme Self drinks the sweet and bitter
Neither liking this nor disliking that.
The ego gropes in darkness, while the Self lives
    in light.
So declared the illumined sages.

(Katha II)

Those who lead an enlightened existence in full Self-awareness are described as 'Those who see all creatures in themselves, and themselves in all creatures' (Isha I). And guidance is provided as to how one may go about attaining such a stage:

The intellect cannot reveal the self,
Beyond its duality of subject
And object. Those who see themselves in all

And all in them, help others through spiritual
Osmosis to realize the Self themselves.
This awakening you have known, comes not
Through logic and scholarship, but from
Close association with a realized teacher.

(Katha II)

So individual guidance from an enlightened teacher is important, and most important of all is meditation. This is expressed repeatedly across the range of Upanishadic texts:

Brahman, the hidden Self in everyone,
Does not shine forth. He is revealed only
To those who keep their minds one-pointed . . .
Meditation enables them to go
Deeper and deeper into consciousness,
From the world of words to the world of thoughts,
Then beyond thoughts to wisdom in the Self.

(Katha II)

At the end of his translation, Easwaran summarizes the essence of the Upanishads with characteristic elegance:

In the end, unity in diversity is not a paradox at all. Unity is the centre . . . of conscious beings, while diversity flourishes on the surface of life. It is as necessary to foster diversity there on the outside as it is to hold unity on the inside.

Diversity is, therefore, as vital as unity; one reflects the other, indeed, necessitates the other. All the different forms of matter and of life, all the sentient beings and all the various gods mythologized in the Hindu tradition, are all thus manifestations of the same single Self.

Through the millennia, this realization has never been lost to us. It has been reflected repeatedly through the ages, all the way down to the popular music and culture of today. And along the way, various teachers have appeared, who have illuminated pathways to the authentic experience of our fundamental nature. One such teacher was a former Indian prince, known as Siddhartha Gautama – the Buddha.

The Buddha was, in many respects, the world's first psychologist. Two and a half thousand years ago, he launched into a quest involving years of extensive and detailed research upon the human mind, and all using a sample size of one – himself. Through meditation, he plunged deep into the inner psyche and there found a place that connects us all.

His subsequent teachings became particularly focused on how one goes about reconnecting to the most fundamental authenticity of our being. He referred to the experience of a world of separation as Maya – something similar to an illusion – to which we can become tied through an intoxication with our senses and thinking mind, known as Mara. His teachings, including core texts like the *Dhammapada*, were focused on guidance and instruction on how to reach through this to what he referred to as 'the other shore':

> If you want to reach the other shore, don't let doubts, passions and cravings strengthen your fetters. Meditate deeply, discriminate between

the pleasant and the permanent, and break the fetters of Mara. (*Dhammapada* XXIV)

It is by going within – 'crossing the river' – that we can rediscover the original ground of our being:

Cross the river bravely; conquer all your passions.
Go beyond the world of fragments and know the deathless ground of life. (*Dhammapada* XXVI)

And the reward for those who do is an unmistakably transformed life; they become what the Buddha described – using the terminology of his ancestors – as a Brahmin:

That one I call a Brahmin who has risen above the duality of this world, free from sorrow and free from sin. Such a one shines like the full moon with no cloud in the sky . . .
    That one I call a Brahmin who is free from 'I', 'me', and 'mine', who knows the rise and fall of life. Such a one is awake and will not fall asleep again. (*Dhammapada* XXVI)

Throughout his teaching, the Buddha was very careful not to conceptualize the nature of the interconnected reality that lay beyond the illusory nature of separation. Any attachment of words to it, he believed, would immediately be limiting. A student once asked him whether or not there was a creator, and he remained entirely silent without answering the question. This occasion – known as Buddha's Noble Silence – contains all the answers that can be given on the subject, for all we can say is what it is not. The minute we attach a word to it, we are using the limitations of language and logic and so instantly treading down a distorted path. This ineffability is a core concept of Eastern mysticism.

Around the time of the Buddha, but further east in China, another spiritual movement, known as Taoism, was formulating a similar understanding of the ultimate reality. In one of Taoism's most important texts – the *Tao Te Ching* – the unknowability of this all-pervading reality, which is referred to as 'Tao', is put front and centre. Indeed, the book opens with the following verse:

> The Tao that can be told is not the eternal Tao
> The name that can be named is not the eternal
>   Name
> The unnameable is the eternally real.
> Naming is the origin of all particular things.
> Free from desire, you realize the mystery.
> Caught in desire you see only the manifestation.
> Yet mystery and manifestations arise from the
>   same source.
> This source is called darkness.
> Darkness within darkness.
> The gateway to all understanding.
>
> (*Tao Te Ching* I)

The Tao as inconceivable void is a central theme that runs throughout the text:

> Look, and it can't be seen.
> Listen, and it can't be heard.
> Reach, and it can't be grasped.
>
> (*Tao Te Ching* XIV)

It goes on to describe, through powerful poetry and metaphor that, though Tao is the essence and root of everything, it is also nothing:

> We join spokes together in a wheel,
> But it is the centre hole
> That makes the wagon move.
> We shape clay into a pot,
> But it is the emptiness inside
> That holds whatever we want.
> We hammer wood for a house,
> But it is the inner space that makes it liveable.
> We work with being,
> But non-being is what we use.
>
> (*Tao Te Ching* XI)

It is because the core of existence is physically intangible that Eastern and esoteric spirituality talk of using means other than logic or language to gain self-realization. However much we try, our mind will never be able to grasp the true everything and nothingness of reality. Though occasional pointers may arise, the actual experience will always be missed. An intellectual appreciation of oneness is not the same as the actual experience of oneness itself. Self-realization, in other words, is something you experience, not something you understand. It can thus only be attained by bypassing words, concepts and thoughts, and turning inward.

One way to understand this is to imagine that all of us are islands, or land masses on the planet. We believe that we are separated from other land masses by all the seas that surround us. But, just like the planet itself, no island is in reality ever disconnected from any other. Below sea level every mass of land on the planet is actually part of a single whole. In order to realize this, therefore – if you were an island yourself – there would be no point in looking outward. All you would see is the sea and what look like other far-off islands. The only way to realize your true nature would be to look within yourself and go deep down, as if excavating layer after layer, until you are at a level where you realize that all this time the sea had created for you a form of illusion.

Going within is thus the key pathway for realizing our true nature, and this is what some of the most ancient schools of spirituality have been teaching for at least the last 5,000 years. A variety of practices have evolved over the years and millions upon millions of people have used them and attained glimpses of a different order of reality as a result – some more deeply than others.

But similar experiences have also occurred in those who have engaged in no such practice at all. Indeed, they were often people who were experiencing great disturbance, emotional pain and turmoil at the same time. For some, going beyond ego was the result of conscious, deliberate and methodical practice over a period of time, yet for others, something similar appeared to arise out of the involuntary experiences of stress, trauma and even chaos.

In the next section we will explore the mechanics of how these awakenings occur, and how the very nature of ego is such that a form of awakening – albeit in a variety of guises – is as likely to occur in the sufferer of mental illness as it is in the seeker of enlightenment.

PART THREE

Waking Up

The Reason for the Human Condition

Chapter 7
Awakening through Awareness

'See the world in a grain of sand, and
heaven in a flower. See infinity in the palm
of your hand, and eternity in an hour.'

William Blake

IN SOME RESPECTS, as I have detailed in previous chapters, science and spirituality can be regarded as two different paths via which we can arrive at the same destination, namely reality at its most fundamental level. However, if we examine the methods used by each, we will also find that there are, in fact, strong parallels between the paths themselves. Though the disciplines are very different, both science and spirituality are actually doing quite similar things when it comes to exploring the underlying nature of things. Science seeks enlightenment by looking at matter on smaller and smaller scales, from masses of matter, to individual atoms, to electrons and the whole subatomic realm. Spiritual practices aimed at achieving enlightenment are also about focusing on the minutiae of life, from a visible object to a reverberating sound, to the mere act of breathing. The spiritual seeker is trained to sustain attention on specific things and, in so doing, gain awareness over time of the reality that lies at its heart.

Both methods are about intense observation of the smallest possible detail. While, for the scientists, this involves complex instrumentation, calculation, and consequent theorizing and conceptualization, for the spiritual seeker it involves pure sensing and experiencing of the object including, indeed highlighting, one's own reaction to that which is being observed – avoiding conceptualization as much as possible. The scientific methods seeks 'objective' means by which to understand the scrutinized object, whereas the spiritual realm focuses on the subjective nature of the experience and how observation of anything intently enough will therefore, in the end, always become an observation of one's self.

Through my own recent spiritual journey, I have explored a number of these spiritual methods myself and – unlike science, which is focused entirely on understanding things through the thinking mind – the common strand in all of these is the active pursuit of a wisdom that is said to exist beyond the thinking mind. For the materialist thinker, wedded to logic, such an idea is, of course, preposterous. As such a person myself, once upon a time, it certainly was to me too. But then that was hardly surprising given that my whole experience of life had been centred around the thinking mind up till that point. Now, however, I see things very differently; I feel that the comedian Emo Phillips made the best observation of all in some respects when he said, 'I used to think the brain was the most important organ in the body, until I realized what was telling me that.'

To those trapped in the realm of thought, therefore, the very notion of such spiritual practices will be nothing short of ridiculous, and that reaction is as far as they will take it. The feeling that the practice might seem silly is, however, also experienced by spiritual seekers, particularly when engaging in it. But the minute they don't give in to that thought or feeling, is when they start to realize that their thinking – often cajoling – mind is not who they really are.

Such practices may involve observing an object for long periods of time, or reciting a particular *mantra* dozens of times, or turning over a single question (like a *koan*) repeatedly, or performing a movement – like walking back and forth – slowly and repetitively, or paying attention to one's breathing. And, every time the mind wanders, one brings the attention back to the object in focus over and over again. These practices are seemingly mundane and repetitive for a reason. The Buddha said, describing what he called the second foundation of mindfulness (I will write more about this in the final section of this book), that whatever we pay attention to will evoke a reaction in us that is either positive, negative or neutral. He then said that whenever something neutral is encountered, if we remove our attention from it, it will eventually be experienced as something negative, but if, on the other hand, we sustain our attention on it, the experience will, over time, become joyful. I know from my own experience that this is exactly what happens. The joy that is ultimately arrived at is so deep because it is uncaused, as far as the logical mind is concerned. You are not happy for a reason – it's not because you got good grades in an exam or bought the latest iPhone – you are just happy, plain and simple. This untethered joy is something very different to the happiness we experience in response to stimulation or positive events, for it is, in fact, the pure joy of being. Just being. And that makes it frightening too. The psychiatrist Mark Epstein explores this experience in his book *Going on Being*:

> The Buddha noticed that there was something scary about this pleasure that appeared out of nowhere. 'Why am I afraid of such pleasure?' he wondered . . . The pleasure feels too great, too undeserved, too blinding. Yet this, as the Buddha intuited, is the direction of enlightenment . . . After a moment's reflection, [he] saw through the fear. A pleasure that did not depend on the gratification of desire was a pleasure inherent to what is . . .
>
> That there could be a happiness unrelated to sensory pleasure at first glance appeared to be impossible, but it is, in fact, a reality, that even Freud, whose focus was sensory pleasure, was forced to admit. While sensory pleasures derive from pursuit of pleasant physical sensations, from the instincts or erotic drives that Freud demonstrated exist even in children, there is another kind of happiness that derives from being in the moment, the joy of aliveness or at-one-ness or concentration.

Epstein then went on to relate his own experience:

> The big surprise to me, even though it was stressed in all the classical texts, was how indispensable feelings of joy were in establishing a foundation

in mindfulness . . . For me, it was this quality more than any other that surprised and delighted me in my early retreats.

The reason that we do not all feel this joy all of the time is the complexity generated by our thinking brain and its ultimate creation – the lens through which it sees the world – ego. Again, as Mark Epstein puts it,

> Why should a pleasure that jumps out of nowhere, not dependent on sensual desires, be frightening? Perhaps because it challenges our identity as someone who is lost, hungry, cut-off, deprived, bereft, searching, or in need.

So long as we are immersed in ego, and the machinations of thought, this joy remains hidden from us. That is why the first goal of all these practices is the dismantling of ego, one brick at a time. That is also why such exercises deliberately provoke the ego: 'This is boring.' 'I have so much else to do.' 'This is crazy.' And on it goes. The practice is never about suppressing such reactions, but noticing them. It is a little like putting cheese in a mouse trap: you want to attract the attention of that which you pursue. And so, in this way, the ego comes out for us to see, in the glaring headlights of awareness. And slowly but surely we begin to realize that we are not that. This 'I' is, in fact, a creation of mind. It is a part of us, but it is not who we are.

This is something you can experiment with right now. As you read this sentence, you may formulate the intention just to sit still for three minutes at the end of this paragraph. That surely won't put you out. If you want to try this then, at the end of the paragraph, set an alarm on your phone or watch, close your eyes and just pay attention to the inner sensations of your breathing: air coming in and out of your nostrils, chest expanding and contracting, diaphragm rising and falling. Just sit still and notice it. This is a gentle trap for ego, as I can almost guarantee that your thinking brain will spring into action. When it does, then just watch it. Every time you notice you're thinking, just watch your thoughts like bubbles. None of them are you. The real you didn't want any of that. The real you just wanted to sit still and observe the breath. Try and return to the breath as often as you can till the three minutes are up.

Doing this helps you realize that the thinking function – and the 'I' it produces – is not the whole you. It is a part of you, but it is the part that thinks it is all of you. When in fact it isn't. And it is the simple act of paying attention to the seemingly mundane that will help you deepen this realization over time. As the composer John Cage once said, 'In Zen they say: if something is boring for two minutes, try it for four. If still boring, try it for eight, sixteen, thirty-two and so on. Eventually one discovers that it's not very boring at all but very interesting.'

These exercises are designed, artfully and gently, to dethrone ego from its position of dominance, and return us to our original state of integrated being. And embedded within this is the authentic experience of joy. Many people who have meditated for a while have had such experiences, and they are so powerful and sometimes overwhelming that this is seen as something that is not just quantitatively different, but qualitatively different from anything they have ever known before. And these experiences often stay in the memory for a long time afterwards.

Anyone who has had such experiences can recognize their authenticity immediately upon hearing of them from others. I was on a train with a woman returning from a meditation retreat once and she described a past experience of intense joy and radiance – the likes of which she had never touched in her life before. The experience appeared to shake her to her core and it had stayed with her ever since, significantly changing her perspective on life. Though her description resonated with me deeply I could easily understand how another person on the train overhearing our conversation might reflexively write it off as 'subjective' or 'mumbo jumbo' – the inevitable consequence of perceiving such things through the lens of ego. I was aware of such reactions within myself too, but I had learnt not to trust them as blindly as I used to. There was a deeper part of me that I was now open to and that knew otherwise.

The idea that such deeper levels of wisdom and knowledge might appear nonsensical to the uninitiated has been known by people who have had such experiences for thousands of years. Perhaps the most famous illustration of this was written by Plato some 2,500 years ago in his famous work *The Republic*:

> Those who are destitute of philosophy may be compared to prisoners in a cave, who are only

able to look in one direction because they are bound, and who have a fire behind them and a wall in front.. Between them and the wall is nothing. All they see is shadows of themselves, and of objects behind them, cast on the wall by the light of the fire. Inevitably they regard these objects as real and have no notion of the objects to which they are due. At last, some man succeeds in escaping from the cave to the light of the sun; for the first time he sees real things and becomes aware that he has hitherto been deceived by shadows. If he is the sort of philosopher who is fit to become a guardian, he will feel it his duty to those who were formerly his fellow prisoners, to go down again into the cave, instruct them as to the truth, and show them the way up. But he will have difficulty in persuading them, because coming out of the sunlight, he will see shadows less clearly, and will seem to them stupider than before his escape.

Plato was pointing to the notion that our senses and the brain that interprets them are not actually showing us reality as it is: it is a version of reality that our thinking self has bound us to. This is very similar to the Buddha's perspective as well. He spoke about how the means to enlightenment were about sustained attention to the experience of your senses which will, over time, allow you to realize the projected nature of everything you experience. Every single thing you perceive is merely a reality that you are interpreting, not one that really exists independently in its own right. And sustained attention to both the object you are viewing and your reaction to it will, over time, teach you that the two are essentially indistinguishable. For example, in the *Udana* – part of the official Pali Canon, the collection of 'Inspired Utterances' of the Buddha – he gives a teaching to a man named Bahiya, who, legend has it, upon hearing it, instantly attained enlightenment:

> In the seen, there is only the seen,
> in the heard, there is only the heard,
> in the sensed, there is only the sensed,
> in the cognized, there is only the cognized.
> Thus you should see that
> indeed there is no thing here;
> this, Bahiya, is how you should train yourself.
> Since, Bahiya, there is for you
> in the seen, only the seen,
> in the heard, only the heard,
> in the sensed, only the sensed,
> in the cognized, only the cognized,
> and you see that there is no thing here,
> you will therefore see that
> indeed there is no thing there.
> As you see that there is no thing there,
> you will see that
> you are therefore located neither in the world of
>   this,
> nor in the world of that,
> nor in any place
> betwixt the two.
> This alone is the end of suffering.
>
> (*Udana* 1: 10)

With time and practice – or sometimes spontaneously, during particularly powerful/moving sense experiences – ego comes face to face with itself and, as soon as it does, it begins to recede. It never permanently disappears, but it steps down from a position in which it was once central to our lives.

Occasionally, though, glimpses of total ego dissolution may occur – little shards of light from the egoless state – and this can feel particularly disorientating. Suddenly, all aspects of the ego perspective dissolve; all concepts, boundaries, perceptions and all notions of space and time collapse. Over a hundred years ago the eminent psychologist William James began cataloguing exactly such experiences, and he went on to publish them in his book *The Varieties of Religious Experience*. One such description is from a J A Symonds:

> Suddenly at church or in company, or when I was reading, and always, I think, when my muscles were at rest, I felt the approach of the mood. Irresistibly it took possession of my mind and will, lasted what seemed an eternity, and . . . resembled the awakening from anaesthetic influence. . . I cannot even now find words to render it intelligible. It consisted of a gradual but swift progressive obliteration of space, time, sensation and the multitudinous factors of experience which seem to qualify what we are pleased to call our self. In proportion, as these conditions of ordinary consciousness were subtracted, the sense of an underlying or essential consciousness acquired intensity. At last, nothing remained

but a pure, absolute, abstract self. The universe became without form and devoid of content. But Self persisted, formidable in its vivid keenness ... And what then? The apprehension of a coming dissolution, the grim conviction that this state was the last state of the conscious Self, the sense that I had followed the last thread of being to the verge of the abyss, and had arrived at a demonstration of eternal Maya or illusion.

Experiences like this have been recorded through the centuries in every continent. I found that, after my own experience, the more I talked about it – which I was, admittedly, sometimes wary of doing – the more people I encountered who had had similar experiences.

Another prominent example is that of Rev. Professor John Hick, a Christian philosopher of religion. A very practical and thoughtful man, Professor Hick describes in his book *The Fifth Dimension* how he usually experiences the world like the rest of us. He is 'here' and the rest of the world is 'out there'. And, like the rest of us, this sense of separation evokes a variety of hopes and fears in him. But one day, after he finished meditating, a completely different experience momentarily came over him: 'I was suddenly aware of being an integral part of the world, not separate from it, and that of which I am a part is a friendly universe, so that there could not possibly be anything to fear or worry about.'

Another particularly articulate description I came across was that of a former Indian businessman by the name of Jaggi Vasudev. In his younger years he was a graduate in English Literature, steeped in European culture, and everything he touched seemed to turn to gold. His businesses went from success to success and, purely to build his own fitness and physical resilience, he also started practising yoga. One day, between business meetings, he climbed a hill near his home town and sat on the hilltop in silence to relax for a while. He recounts what happened next in lectures he now gives around the world:

> Till that moment in my life I always thought this is me and that's somebody else and something else. But [for] the first time I did not know which is me and which is not me. Suddenly, what was me was just all over the place. The very rock on which I was sitting, the air that I breathe, the very atmosphere around me, I had just exploded into everything. That sounds like utter insanity. I thought this madness lasted for ten to fifteen minutes, but when I came back to my normal consciousness, four-and-a-half-hours had passed. I was sitting there, fully conscious, eyes wide open since three o'clock in the afternoon, and it was now seven-thirty, yet I thought only ten minutes had passed. For the first time in my adult life, tears were flowing to the point where my shirt is completely wet. Me and tears were impossible . . . I am bursting with another kind of ecstasy which is indescribable. Every cell in my body is just bursting with ecstasy. When I shook my skeptical mind and asked it what is happening to me? The only thing that my mind could tell me was 'maybe

you are going off your rocker'. I didn't care what it was but I didn't want to lose it, because this was the most beautiful thing that I had ever touched, and I had never imagined that a human being could ever feel like this within himself.

These experiences can occur spontaneously in people of all backgrounds, regardless of spiritual or philosophical leanings. Alan Smith, a physician and biomedical researcher who was also a self-confessed reductionist scientist, also had such an experience while watching a particularly beautiful sunset from his home in Oakland, California. As the light in the sky became extremely bright, he began to notice a sense of time slowing down. Then suddenly,

I merged with the light and everything, including myself, becoming one unified whole. There was no separation between myself and the rest of the universe . . . there was neither 'subject' nor 'object.' All words or discursive thinking had stopped and there was . . . just a timeless, unitary state of being.

As truly remarkable and explosive as these experience are, it is often their consequences that are most noticeable to the people around them. Life becomes filled with a new sense of meaning and purpose and the seeker often finds himself travelling in all sorts of new directions. An energy and verve accompanies the changed perspective and, again, this is something I can attest to myself, in my own small way. I used to sleep a regular average seven or eight hours every night. I occasionally experienced the odd night of mild insomnia – maybe a couple of times a month – when I would get no more then about four or five hours' sleep, and this tended to have a profound effect on me the next day, leaving me lacking in energy and concentration and with a wholly unpleasant, even wretched, feeling inside.

After I started to have these experiences in my meditation practice, however, four or five hours a night became my norm. This worried me at first but, over time, I noticed that something else had dramatically shifted underneath. Instead of feeling like I somehow lacked sleep, I realized that I was waking up after four hours, feeling exactly as I used to after seven or eight. I didn't get particularly tired, or low in feeling or concentration – it just felt natural. Now I often find myself creeping out of bed at around four in the morning before going for a jog, meditating and starting my day. It took me a while to work out the reason for this, and then I came across an explanation that resonated perfectly in Adyashanti's book *The End of Your World*:

> When we realize the true nature of existence – when existence itself has awakened to itself – there is almost always an energetic component to the realization. By energetic component, what I mean is that there is a profound realignment of the way our system works. A type of rewiring occurs in the mind at the mental level, and there is a rewiring of how we sense and perceive on an emotional level . . .
>
> In many ways it is only in retrospect that we come to understand that the dream state itself, the

state of egoic separation, chews up tremendous amounts of energy. Only once it dissolves can we see the immense amount of energy required to continue the perception of separation that most of us live with. While we're in it, we have no sense just how much energy is being spent on the dream of separation. You may have certain moments of suffering or despair, and in those moments you can feel how the perception of separation is draining your energy. But it is only when consciousness has spontaneously freed itself from the dream state that there is a huge internal release - mostly because the blocks are no longer there.

So the ego requires vast amounts of energy to prop itself up and, therefore, once it is diminished, and no longer sits at the centre of our world, great reservoirs of energy become released. Adyashanti goes on to say,

> One of the most common things that happens as the energy starts to open up within us is insomnia . . . This does not mean that anything has gone wrong. The whole energy of the body is realigning itself; it's coming into a different state of harmony.

Over time, this extra energy becomes channelled into constructive outlets. For me, of course, it is this book, my new perspectives on mental health, and the work that flows from it. Alan Smith quit his job as a university academic, despite having won a national prize for the research he conducted. He found he had less anxiety in general and was able to enjoy life more working as a part-time clinician, giving him more time to explore issues relating to consciousness, spirituality and mysticism. Jaggi Vasudev also channelled his energies toward a new-found spiritual calling. He started to tour the country to teach yoga to others and, over time, he came to be known as Sadhguru. He is now one of the most popular spiritual gurus in India, and has taught his unique spiritual practice – Isha Yoga – to over two million people around the world.

Another truly inspiring example is that of Dr Edgar Mitchell. Dr Mitchell, a graduate of MIT, was one of the Apollo 14 astronauts – the sixth man to walk on the moon. On the return journey from the moon he had an experience that changed his entire perspective on life:

> I realized that the molecules of my body and my partners, and the molecules of the spacecraft were prototyped in some ancient generation of stars. And suddenly, instead of being an intellectual experience, it was an emotional experience, followed with an ecstasy! So my question was: Wow! What kind of a brain/body is this that causes this sort of experience?
>
> It was only after I came back to earth and started researching the mystical literature that I realized that the experience that I was having all the way back home had a name. It's called *samadhi* in the ancient Sanskrit — the *samadhi* experience. That's pretty wild!
>
> Many of my compatriots, like Charlie Duke and Jim Irwin in particular, had very much the

same experience, but they described it as looking on the face of God, which is a traditional, mystical or religious way of expressing such experiences. Others came back and began to express their sense of personal amazement and emotion through creativity – painting and poetry, for example.

The experience was evidently shared by several of the astronauts and each found a channel through which to celebrate their realization. For Mitchell, the path that lay ahead for him was clear:

It . . . made me realize that our story of ourselves, as taught by our science, is largely incomplete, and perhaps flawed. And our story of ourselves, as taught by our religious cosmology, is archaic and most certainly flawed. So the point is, since we are now a space-faring civilization, maybe we'd better re-answer those questions . . . It's given me a life's work of trying to understand the nature of consciousness.

Mitchell went on to become the founder of the Institute of Noetic Sciences, a research institute like no other. Their website reminds us that '"Noetic" comes from the Greek word *nous*, which means "intuitive mind" or "inner knowing."' And their mission is 'supporting individual and collective transformation through consciousness research, educational outreach, and engaging a global learning community in the realization of our human potential'.

Through communities such as the Institute of Noetic Sciences, spiritual teachers, gurus, friends and fellow travellers, I have come to understand the process of awakening through awareness. This is a step-by-step dismantling of ego that can have a transformative effect on an individual's life, her vision of the world and her role within it. But in the parallel experiences of my patients, I have also come to understand a very different pathway to awakening: One that, though no less authentic, can also be clouded by what appears to be a simultaneous expansion of ego. It is in this context that I will re-examine the phenomena of psychological distress and mental illness in the chapters ahead.

Chapter 8

Ego Inflammation

'One of the symptoms of an approaching nervous breakdown is the belief that one's work is terribly important.'

Bertrand Russell

IN MY ACUTE HOSPITAL WARD, the proportion of people admitted for treatment of severe mental illness who have experienced trauma or abuse in some shape or form in their earlier lives is vast; I estimate it to be easily over 90%. Most mental illness, in fact, whether severe or mild – or even just basic psychological stress – is strongly linked with life events: losses, mishaps, and the strains of life. None of this is surprising, of course. Nowadays, we all take for granted the fact that life stressors can make us vulnerable to emotional and mental instability. But very rarely do we stop to question why this is, or rather how exactly it comes about. How do specific events like bereavement, divorce or job loss, for example – which will understandably generate a particular set of reactions concerning those events – then become generalized into more global experiences of stress, anxiety or depression? How does a specific experience of emotional pain spread out to become such broad-based suffering?

The answer lies in the fact that we happen to experience all these events through the lens of ego. This happened 'to me', or that happened 'because of me', or even this happened 'in front of me' or that happened 'to someone who knows me'. Every experience is related, in one way or another, to 'me'. The thinking mind, with its sole ability to process data through the concept of ego, can only perceive things in relation to this ego. Ego and thinking mind, therefore, become indistinguishable. This is why there is no language that you can use to describe any event you have ever encountered without in some way, during the course of that description – explicitly or implicitly – referencing it to yourself. Right away, therefore, all your experiences of life will automatically have an effect on this 'me'. Sometimes the effect will be positive, and other times it will be negative.

Furthermore, the thinking mind can only process experiences by attaching words to them: 'happy', 'sad', 'good, 'bad', 'nasty' and so on. This way, every experience becomes attached to a judgement. This judgement is then added, by association, to the notion of 'I'. As the ego is just a series of concepts and judgements to start with – descriptions or stories strung together to formulate our sense of self – as soon as we add these new lines to it, the whole sense of 'I' becomes changed. It is like adding a word to a sentence. It will always, in some way, change the meaning of the sentence. An experience, in other words, becomes like putting dye into water – the whole body of fluid will be affected.

Our sense of self is thus an ever-shifting entity, as every encounter we have alters it. Just as throwing a stone into a lake will affect the whole lake, so subjecting the ego to an experience will affect the whole ego. That is why our ego is so inherently unstable, and it explains why so many of us feel like we're never more than two steps away from a nervous breakdown much of the time.

Our problem is not that we have an ego, but that we believe it is the sum total of who we are. And because we do, we are forever strapped in to its way of working, like a frightened child on a roller coaster. Our ego is forever fighting a rearguard action to defend its territory – the definitions and stories upon which it rests – as it is being challenged almost every waking hour. And it does this by engaging in activities that reinforce the notions upon which it is founded. These notions are sometimes not conscious, but they are there nonetheless. For example, a common attribute many of our egos possess, deep down inside, is the idea that we are 'stressed' or, in some way 'unhappy' in the modern world. Ego then goes about reinforcing this inner sense of unease paradoxically by trying to avoid feeling 'stressed' or 'unhappy'. It does this by going out of its way to deny many of the feelings that are generated inside when we encounter difficult situations. We all do it. Rarely do we sit with the pain we are feeling when something doesn't go our way (as is often the case) – paying attention to the experience in our body – and giving it some space and time. Instead we go into avoidance mode. We keep ourselves busy, we think, we act, we talk, we eat, we work, we do whatever we can to zone out; engaging in these activities is almost a form of anaesthesia. But this itself then generates more stress and makes us more unhappy.

Avoidance of the thing it defines itself as is, in fact, the most powerful route through which ego reinforces those same attributes. And the more we indulge these machinations, the more inflamed our ego becomes, and the vicious cycle goes on.

This is indeed the foundation of neurotic disorders. The anorexic sufferer, for example, starts with the idea that 'I' am overweight, even though this is usually not the case. I remember spending a whole session, in my fledgling days as a junior doctor in psychiatry, trying to convince a poor young woman with anorexia that she was not in fact overweight. Even though she was clearly underweight, my persuasion didn't make any difference to her. The thought was still there. It was now part of her ego story. This then leads to marked behaviours to avoid being overweight, which then – because they are being engaged in much of the time, and with such dedication and focus – paradoxically serve to reinforce further the notion 'I am overweight.' The thought creates the behaviour, but then the behaviour, which is always carried out with the persistent thought in mind, serves to reinforce the thought. The consequences of this vicious cycle can, of course, be tragic. Some studies suggest that up to 20% of people who suffer anorexia ultimately die of the illness.

A similar pattern occurs in obsessive compulsive disorder where the ego is built on a foundation of, for example, 'I am dirty.' This may be a physical or a metaphoric sense of 'dirtiness' that became entangled in the ego story somewhere along the line, and it results in the sufferer going to extreme lengths to avoid all dirt, like bathing and washing hands dozens of times a day. The perpetual duty of such an ego becomes to clean, which, paradoxically, only serves to keep the idea of being dirty alive. OCD can relate to a host of repetitive ruminations, and the ritualistic behaviours that sometimes flow from them – such as checking things, following elaborate routines and switching things on and off – are all means via which the ego paradoxically reinforces feelings that have become deeply entrenched within the underlying concept of 'I', like 'I am in danger,' 'I am unlucky,' or 'I lose control.'

Similarly, the person with acute anxiety or panic attacks believes he is going to die. This fear is so great that it generates a set of physical manifestations that leave the sufferer feeling like they really are about to die, by experiencing a heart attack or something similarly fatal. One sufferer once put it to me that 'It feels like I am on board a plane hurtling towards the ground in the last seconds of my life.' The fear of imminent death itself generates symptoms akin to those of impending death, thereby keeping the fear of death alive. And for phobias the fear is often of losing control, being embarrassed or humiliated.

In post-traumatic stress disorder, the memory of the traumatic event itself has become embedded into the ego. The powerful nature of the trauma burns its way into the ego story, like some sort of deep scar and, as a result, the sufferer finds himself avoiding anything that generates the memory. But the more avoidance he engages in, the more the memory becomes firmly embedded in the ego story – inflaming it further – and, as a result, the more of life he needs to avoid. This can lead to major breakdowns as the sufferer backs away into smaller and smaller corners, leaving his life to become more and more restricted.

All of these phenomena lead to avoidance, and this avoidance becomes their fuel. The various constructs of ego proliferate as powerful thoughts settle into the mind, like the stories of an unstable skyscraper, swaying precariously in the wind.

The larger the ego grows the less secure it is, until ultimately chinks start to appear on its surface. This is when a phenomenon occurs that is known to psychiatrists as depersonalization. Depersonalization occurs with neurotic disorders of any description – particularly panic attacks – but it can also occur on its own. In the psychiatrists' diagnostic guidebook, the *DSM* (*Diagnostic and Statistical Manual*), depersonalization is described as an 'alteration in the perception or experience of the self so that one feels detached from and as if one is an outside observer of one's mental processes or body'. This is, in many respects, akin to that which is described as an out-of-body experience. Here are some quotes from people who have experienced depersonalization, cited in the case study literature. It's worth noting that none of these experiences occurred within the context of any drug use:

> I don't know who I am — of course I am [name] but I feel like a robot, like I am listening to someone else talking, like I am looking at myself from the outside, but it is not another voice or body – it is mine, it is me, it just doesn't feel like it . . . I

spend all day trying to figure it out. Maybe I am too analytical.

This sounds mad but I am not me. I look in the mirror and I don't see me. I don't know who it is that I see and I don't know where the real me has gone. Logically that cannot be the case, but that is how it feels. I spend all day checking myself and it's never me.

One day I was walking around the city, minding my own business, when suddenly I found myself looking down at myself from somewhere near the awning of a store. It was unreal and the weirdest thing in the world . . . Since then, and that was 20 years ago, I've had one experience like that after another and never completely felt like I was back in my body. I constantly feel spaced out.

From an awakening perspective, this is where it appears that ego has lost control. People who experience depersonalization are, in that moment, no longer stuck in an awareness that is solely filtered through the prism of ego – it is as if their awareness has popped out and expanded beyond the narrow confines of 'I'. But because it was not actively sought or gradually worked towards, it is also usually experienced as a disturbing and frightening event. Such experiences are, nevertheless, remarkably common. Symptoms of depersonalization have a reported prevalence rate of up to 20%, though many don't report it for fear of being told that they're 'going mad'. The founder of Acceptance and Commitment Therapy (ACT), Professor Steven Hayes, also suffered panic disorder in his earlier years and he too had this experience: 'I found it so intense and beyond what I could language about . . . It started with a heart attack. I thought I was dying. I thought I was having a heart attack instead of a panic attack – and [I had] this sense of stepping out and watching my hand reach out to call the emergency room.' He then reacted to this out-of-body experience by, 'howling my way into the moment and kind of landing, and then making a promise to myself that no matter what happens I was not going to turn away from that experience . . . and that puts me on the path that leads me into the ACT world.'

The experience shook him so profoundly that he started to re-examine his whole understanding of the self and the thinking mind and, as a result, he embarked upon a new course of research that ultimately led to the formulation of one of the fastest-growing therapies in the world of psychology and mental health today.

So in the process of breaking down, we are sometimes able to glimpse that which is beyond. Without naming it or attaching labels to it, we realize that there is a wider awareness that we are a part of that stretches way beyond the small 'I' through which we saw the world up to that point. The ego begins to collapse under its own weight. And this is a trajectory that we all have a propensity to move toward. Indeed, that is one of the key definitions of neurotic disorders – they are a quantitative, rather than qualitative departure from the norm. In other words, we all have elements of this process going on inside us. We all experience our thinking mind going into overdrive from time to time. We all experience insecurity and fear as a result of buying into it, and we all experience moments of peace and space when the whirlwind is spontaneously suspended – like a record player suddenly coming to a halt after a power cut – and we sense, if even for a millisecond, that what we think is not all there is; that there is a knowing beyond that which the 'I' can tell us. Any memory or interpretation of the experience is often wiped away soon after, though. Our 'I' just can't handle it.

In some circumstances, indeed, this break in ego happens so acutely that it ignites a ferocious backlash. As a result, severe depression, bipolar or psychotic disorders may follow, and it is to these major mental illnesses that I will turn in the next chapter.

Chapter 9
Awakening through Suffering

'Only when all our hold on life is troubled,
only in spiritual terror can the truth come
through the broken mind.'

W B Yeats

SOME LIFE EXPERIENCES are so intense and severe that most people who experience them will have a major breakdown as a result. Child sex abuse is one such example: some studies have reported rates of childhood physical and sexual abuse in up to 50% of adolescents and adults with a psychiatric diagnosis. Trauma and abuse in childhood is, therefore, a key predisposing factor to major mental illness. This may take a variety of forms, from neglect to deprivation to high levels of intra-family conflict. Of course, major mental illness can also develop in people who have experienced no such backgrounds and that is when additional predisposing factors will come into play like genetic influences and growth and development of the foetus in the uterus. In most people a combination of these factors underpins the underlying vulnerability.

When trying to understand the early environmental triggers, like a lot of psychiatrists I spend some time attempting to discover exactly what those early experiences were and how they may have impacted on the sufferer psychologically. Every event we encounter in our lives is met with a psychological reaction, and in childhood this reaction is often reflexive. So, for example, a child who is physically abused on a regular basis by her carers may well start to associate this experience of violence with her own sense of self. Abusive relationships or self-harm may then follow in adulthood as a consequence. The tragic idea that establishes itself is that the 'I' is someone who is abused.

This is, indeed, how depression occurs. A study in 2004 involving nearly 10,000 people examined the relationship between adverse childhood experiences – termed ACEs – and depression in later life. They used a score – the ACE score – to quantify the extent of trauma or abuse a child experienced, and they found a clear correlation between that score and levels of depression in adulthood. 'We found a strong, dose–response relationship between the ACE score and the probability of lifetime and recent depressive disorders.' In other words, the greater the trauma, the more likely it was that the child would grow up to become depressed. This shows the extent to which the concept of 'I' is a story that evolves out of the experiences of our earlier years, and when this 'I' is poisoned from the outset, a high risk of mental illness becomes built into the system. The person will then grow up with a propensity to attach any subsequent negative events to this 'I' too – while avoiding positive ones. So, if two members of the family row, it quickly starts to feel like 'my fault', or if, on the other hand, the person performs an act of kindness, it is quickly rationalized away, 'Oh, anyone would have done the same.'

It's not just abuse or trauma that can lead to this pattern of thinking, of course. Adverse psychological reactions in childhood may be the consequence of all sorts of experiences that inadvertently serve to plant a thick layer of negativity within the notion of 'I'. In fact we will all have this to some degree. No parent can ever be fully attentive to their child all of the time and the very nature of childhood means that anxiety, insecurity and loss will inevitably be experienced. As a result – to a greater or lesser extent – we all walk round with these negative feelings attached to our sense of self, which then form the basis of judgements lurking under the surface, waiting like a magnet to pick up any adverse experience and attach it to the 'I' too. A vicious cycle can then be triggered in which an increasingly negative 'I' develops a stronger and stronger gravitational pull for every negative event it encounters, incorporating them all, one after the other: 'I'm stupid.' 'It's all my fault, I just know it is.' And eventually, if this carries on long enough, the ego develops so much mass that it starts to collapse in on itself like a dense star forming a black hole: 'I wish I was never born.' From here, without further protective factors outside the ego – like friends, family or prohibiting religious or ethical beliefs – it can be a few short steps to 'I want to die.'

The ego is dissolving, and as it was not a process that was sought, planned or gradually worked towards – with any awareness of a reality beyond ego – the experience becomes a frightening and distressing one. Nevertheless, for many people, this dissolution also brings about a peek over the wall of the ego paradigm to the potential that lies on the other side of it. There are many stories of a sense of spiritual union slowly blossoming within people who experience depression, particularly when gaps in the monologue of the now exhausted mind arise. One former sufferer told me of a powerful sense – in the midst of his severe depression – that he, along with the rest of creation, was the materialization of a single divine source that manifested through each of us. Another spoke of sitting on a beach, watching waves for hours on end as the whirlwind of the mind came to a halt and gave way to a distant, yet familiar, feeling of the divine all around. Experiences like this are often overlooked by those caring for someone with depression but, in my estimation, they are actually a lot more common than most people realize.

As the ego, for the first time, runs out of energy, like a car spluttering to a halt, new experiences of reality start to emerge. A French professor of psychology, Marc-Alain Descamps, describes the potential contained within this moment:

> In the end, I find it is also possible to speak of the benefits of depression, since not everything is negative. This great suffering, this total despair, can produce something good . . .
>
> Something gets started which must not be opposed or stopped. A transformative process is at work and at the beginning requires a new start: this is the cleaning aspect of depression . . .

One need not hurry, and instead can wait for time to complete its work, and a new way of seeing things to develop. Which things? The world and its destiny, to start with, but then especially oneself. Depression can give birth to a new being, and therefore it can be considered as the price to pay to be able to change.

For some, however, the ego paradigm, which has been hard-wired from the earliest of years, does not relinquish its grip easily. A further backlash may then plunge the patient deeper into the depths of depression. What is sometimes known as a retarded depression can occur, where the sufferer disengages almost completely from life – even neglecting basic levels of self-care like washing or eating – or, alternatively, the mind may paradoxically shift gear into a higher level of activity, fuelling the inner restlessness of what is known as an agitated depression, or even a mixed anxiety depression. Suicide can also become a risk. The ego's ability to annihilate itself, rather than face dethronement is a possibility that should not be overlooked in severe cases.

Alternatively, with the right combination of environmental cues and brain chemistry, the thinking mind may swing the mood into the opposite direction and an episode of mania may then ensue, turning it into what is conventionally referred to as a bipolar disorder.

It has been known since the days of Freud that a manic mood is often a form of defence against the opposite – a dark depressed insecurity that the mind is working overtime to deny. In the flurry of activity that takes place, the mind races, bombarding the sufferer with an assortment of ideas, schemes and plans. There is an unstoppability and an irrepressibility to mania, meaning that sleep becomes increasingly hard to come by, and sentences increasingly hard to finish. The agitated mind is, again, breaking down, almost as if it were cannibalizing itself, and as a result thick cracks in the ego shell emerge. A new light starts to seep in, and this can often merge with the symptoms of the over-active mind itself, so that most clinicians will simply chalk all such expressions down to the ramblings of a manic mind.

One of many such accounts of this kind of experience, and psychiatry's reaction to it, is by an articulate medical professional himself. In a recollection of his own manic episode, Dr Edward Whitney described feeling 'overwhelmed by a sense of angelic presences', and a feeling that 'fear and hatred would rule no longer. God would no longer be a tool of oppression. With my entire being, I wanted this to be true.' None of this made any sense to his clinical carers, however, who could only understand it through the prism of psychiatric diagnosis. 'The mental health care system and I were at cross purposes; what I was experiencing as a wonderful healing process was construed by my doctors as a serious disease process. Neither of us had a clue about the other's perspective.' Nevertheless, he ultimately concluded that, 'Mania, in my experience of it, is a process of giving birth to hope in the soul.' But, at the same time, he was equally clear about the negative energy with which such an experience is juxtaposed. 'It is opposed from within by an equally intense nihilism and fear that the entire creation is nothing more than a cesspool of doom.'

In mood disorders, therefore, a pre-existing vulnerability, often from early life experience, can set an ego up with a Velcro surface, sensitive and primed for life's negative experiences to stick to it. Over time, it gradually builds itself up to the point where it starts to collapse under its own weight, producing the distressing symptoms of depression and/or mania – a hyperactive mind, dragging the sufferer down or up (or both) – while sometimes simultaneously presenting her with glimpses of what lies beyond. If the sufferer is in any way able to connect to it authentically, through all the disabling fog of illness, then a feeling of some form of spiritual union may occur and, for those in whom it does, a deeper sense of purpose behind their whole journey begins to take shape.

There are more profound levels of dysfunction, however, into which the ego can dive and this tends to occur – whether as a consequence of mood disorders or directly – in those who have a further vulnerability to psychotic illness. Again, this predisposition is generally determined by a combination of hereditary factors and early life experience. In terms of the latter, a multitude of traumatic experiences can contribute, but all of them, in my view, relate in one way or another to an incomplete formation of the logic-bound ego paradigm that the rest of us formulate early on in life and take for granted thereafter.

While most of us suffer from a tunnel vision – seeing the world only through the binoculars of ego – the person with a vulnerability to psychosis never developed a fully formed ego perspective in the first place. Though the ego paradigm has many pitfalls and drawbacks, and total reliance on it is ultimately toxic, an ego that is incompletely formed in the first place is also dangerous, leaving the individual vulnerable to subsequent psychotic breakdown.

Buddhists have a saying, that you have to be somebody before you can be nobody. In other words, humans need to have a fully formed ego before they can learn to connect to the reality beyond it. The problem for the sufferer of psychosis is that, though they may have a greater propensity to connect to that which lies beyond the ego paradigm, as they do not have one foot anchored in it to start with, they are prone to high levels of imbalance. As these notions started coming together for me, they were helped along the way by a truly inspiring *dharma* teacher by the name of Yanai Postelnik. During a 1:1 session in a retreat, I remember him telling me, in his characteristically witty tones and thick New Zealand accent, 'On one level, you and I are indeed one. But if I try and feed you my lunch, then we have a problem!'

Yanai had observed psychosis himself, on a couple of occasions, in the people he had taught at Gaia House and over the years he reached the conclusion that the difference between them and his other students was that those vulnerable to psychosis were not fully grounded in the world we live in to start with. Though the Buddha said that the world we see around us is like an illusion, he nevertheless always taught of its importance and value and how, indeed, it was only through a truly deep, authentic experience of this level of reality that we are able properly to experience that which is beyond it.

My own perspective, therefore, is that people who are vulnerable to psychosis have, through a combination of nature and nurture, not developed a full shell of ego in their earliest years. Where environmental factors come into play, high levels of intra-familial conflict or contradiction appear central. Something called Relational Frame Theory (RFT) has helped me understand this. RFT has managed to unearth some fundamental rules of language and logic. There are certain kinds of assumptions we make all the time when we humans communicate with each other, and the rules that govern these assumptions form the bedrock upon which our ability to use language and logic stands. These rules are taught to us in childhood through a process of reward, trial and error. When the right combination of words or the correct application of logic is demonstrated the child is rewarded with the parent's approval. This needs to be a consistent process. Where conflict or disorder reigns within the household, however, the process becomes hampered. For example, suppose a mother tells her child that left is left and right is right. The father, who has an almost universally confrontational relationship with the mother, then tells the child the same, but also adds that the child's mother is always wrong because she never knows what she is talking about. What is the child then to believe? Or perhaps the mother tells the child that up is up and down is down. The child then repeats this to the father who, being in a bad mood, reproaches the child without listening to what she said, telling her she is an idiot like her know-nothing mother. Again, what conclusions is the child to draw from this? The long-term effect of such regularly paradoxical feedback will be that the whole scaffolding of language and logic is constructed weakly. As a result, the notion of the self – the main creation of language and logic – will also be fragile.

This is why, in my experience, abusive or traumatic relationships make children vulnerable to psychosis. Later in life, however, not everyone with this background will go on to become psychotic. Positive experiences like relationships with friends, work, purpose or partners may well be reparative, but poor relationships or further trauma or abuse can then push the young adult over the edge into a psychotic breakdown. Stimulant drugs are another route. This is also why the majority of people who take cannabis, for example, do not become psychotic as a result, but studies show that a small percentage will, and these are the people who have a pre-existing vulnerability to psychotic breakdown.

It must be stressed at this point, however, that some people become psychotic without any drug use or parenting/relationship problems within the home environment; these are just risk factors, as for smoking and heart disease. But, just like that example, they are strong risk factors and a series of them, including genetic factors, often interact to lead a person down the road of psychosis.

The fragility of ego in the person vulnerable to psychosis means that subsequent stressful life events can trigger what might be called an inflammation relatively easily. This may involve the kind of neurotic or mood-related processes described previously. The insecure ego, in order to protect itself, starts to flare up in one of these directions – just like a piece of skin that is disturbed by something in its environment. If the ego is particularly fragile, then a full break with reality may then occur, which is the phenomenon of psychosis. Again, the analogy with skin applies. When skin becomes inflamed as a result of trauma, it can also start to develop cracks on the surface; there is a simultaneous process of destruction and inflammation, just like the traumatized ego, which both cracks and swells at the same time. This is why, I believe, psychosis is such a paradoxical state. On the one hand, the person is really touching the kind of experience many spiritual adherents seek, a reality outside the linguistically describable or logically definable reality, beyond the confines of ego and thinking mind, but on the other hand they are also experiencing a severe revolt from the ego that manifests as a variety of psychiatric symptoms. Ego is engaged in a ferocious battle, not unlike the way in which white blood cells in the body build up in response to an invasion of foreign matter. To protect itself, the ego starts to stretch and metamorphose so that the sufferer cannot see beyond it. It needs to make a lot of effort to do this, however, and so a dance ensues as the unanchored ego contorts itself into all manner of shapes.

This was encapsulated perfectly by a very intelligent young man I was looking after recently. He had just emerged from a severe psychotic episode and he said that in it he had experienced a strong sense of a 'gentleness about the universe'. I should add at this point that the patient concerned was an atheist with no religious beliefs whatsoever, but he said he felt a strong sense of an 'almost spiritual kind of kindness' around him. He said that he felt he could communicate with wise beings and felt embraced and warmly held by the whole experience. However, he had also done some disturbing things during the experience, things that offended and frightened others – hence his admission to my ward – and they were all behaviours that he would never normally have engaged in. So I asked him about this and how it fitted together with the descriptions above. He said, 'You see doctor, there is a dual aspect to this.' On the one hand there was the positively joyful and uplifting side of the experience but then, at the same time, it was accompanied with 'a great fear', a turmoil and a darkness. Something within him, he believed, seemed to be resisting the process.

As I looked back to how he presented when he was first admitted to our unit, I realized that what I was witnessing was an ego in full self-preservation mode, causing profound suffering to the individual and all those around him, in an attempt to shut out the waves of a deeper reality that were impinging on a domain it had formerly ruled. One could almost visibly see his ego struggling with the light. And I realized then that, if I could somehow help this man build resilience against the inevitable storms of ego in such moments, and so divert him from the suppressions – physical and chemical – that are the unfortunate, yet, inescapable tools of the acute psychiatric system, then a teacher of true wisdom could be born.

Such a 'dual process' is not unique to this case; indeed, it is a fundamental characteristic of psychosis in all its forms and in all who suffer it. A core definition of psychosis is that it represents a breakdown of the barrier between self and non-self. In this very aspect, we can see evidence of both sides of psychosis. The breakdown of this barrier is precisely the basis of the awakening experience, but the insecure ego grabs it and, instead of allowing it to be an experience of oneness with every-thing – where there is no 'I', there is only what is – it converts it into an experience where the 'I' is being invaded by the voices and thoughts of 'the other'. This is why someone with auditory hallucinations will hear his own thoughts and believe that someone else is speaking them. This is how the beautiful is metamorphosed into the terrible. He will believe that inanimate objects talk to him and, in the paranoid state, he will ascribe thoughts and motives to other people and objects that, in all likelihood, he has himself.

The ego has captured the blurring boundary and made it concrete again. So much so, in fact, that people with psychosis often believe what they are saying with a far greater certainty and intensity than most of the rational beliefs that they and the rest of society possess. This is why challenging them can often make them worse. They are the straws to which the disintegrating ego clutches and so they will be clung to with all of ego's might. Sometimes when I try, as tactfully as possible, to explain to a patient why they are in hospital and receiving treat-ment, they look upon me with such disbelief, and some-times disgust, that it is clear that they think I am the one who is confused. Sometimes they say it to me explicitly, 'You're the one who should be in here not me!'

Recently, for example, one patient described to me how his father – who lives in South America, and with whom he has no contact – was giving him instructions to commit acts of violence. I asked him about his father and where exactly he was, and he said, 'My father is everywhere. He knows everything, and he can do anything he likes.' He believed that he, along with the rest of society was bound to do his father's bidding and the acts of violence he was committing were all part of his father's will, a grand plan to which he had wholly surrendered. The fact that I was even questioning this – let alone trying to treat him for it – was a ridiculous notion to him. Despite the acts of violence, he saw his father as a benevolent ruler who was doing all of this for the world's benefit and would ultimately reward everyone who experienced his violence.

Here we see not only the certainty of belief, but also the extent to which his delusional system is heavily laced with spiritual connotations. He is describing a relationship with an omnipresent, omniscient, omnipotent source, but his ego has hijacked it and tied it up into a series of ideas that have returned it once again to a concrete conceptualized reality.

It must be noted, incidentally, that violence and aggression are rare – in absolute terms – among people with psychosis, or mental illness in general. Nevertheless, they still occur at a slightly higher rate than in the general public. The thrashing ego does have the capacity to attack when the new-found reality upon which it hangs its existence is challenged; it must force the new reality into being. It is also why, both in psychosis, and mental illness more generally, the family, carers or people around the patient may experience a challenging or confrontational attitude, or sometimes the opposite, a withdrawal or lack of connection. Ego is desperate to keep the reality shared by society at bay. In some ways we are all hijacked by our egos, but in mental illness, particularly in acute presentations, this is more so than ever.

As it slips out of the reality the rest of society accepts, ego frantically builds up its own cocoon. But because it is stretching itself further and further, gaps inevitably start to form, which then let rays of wider consciousness seep in. As a result this new version of reality is regularly peppered with notions similar to those articulated by mystics through the ages. Examples of this are so common in acute psychiatry that I don't even have to look further back than the day on which I am writing this to find one. Here is the description – again, edited to hide his identity – of a patient I saw only this morning:

> He came to the realization, over recent days, that he was a king, and that it was time for him to fulfil his destiny. As he walked around town, every-thing in the environment acknowledged his right to rule. As people walked their dogs, the dogs stopped to acknowledge him and their owners bowed down to him. The birds all sang songs for him and everyone on the TV and radio knew that it was his time to rule . . . He stared intently at the policewoman standing outside the door, who had brought him into hospital, and said

that he could see her bowing to him. Apparently, he had recently been fired from work, but he was not troubled by this, as he believed it was a fulfilment of his destiny.

So again we see how his delusional system has become mixed up with a sense of power, joy and connection with all. His ego has constructed a world that draws heavily from an expanded consciousness that seems to have been breaking through his former sense of self. He is no longer the circumscribed, finite disconnected ego that he once believed he was, but his ego has imposed itself upon this experience of a more unitary reality and morphed it into a grandiose delusion.

Additional layers of meaning also exist within each constellation of psychotic phenomena that relate particularly to the individual's personal story. I have treated a number of young men who experienced sexual abuse in their childhoods and subsequently developed delusions as adults that people were coming into their houses at night and sexually abusing them in their sleep. Some of them also became more broadly paranoid, with a homophobic tinge, believing that most people around them were gay and therefore should be avoided. It was almost as if they had somehow become stuck in the moment of their abuse – so ingrained was it into their sense of self and the reality that derived from it – like a stuck record constantly replaying the same groove.

As everyone's ego is different, and a product of the life led up to that point, the experience of its disintegration will be different for everyone too. Ego is like a house made out of different materials and designs for each of us. As it starts to collapse in on itself, the pattern of light that enters will be a product of the amount of roof that gives way and the size and shape of hole it leaves behind. The light that enters is thus distorted, and the pattern experienced inside is a combination of the light itself and the material gaps through which it passes. This is how the experience of higher consciousness becomes fundamentally intertwined with an abused and, thus, overgrown, collapsing ego.

The negative symptoms of schizophrenia are said to be a withdrawal from engagement with the world in general. Basic activities and life skills are lost and even thought itself becomes slowed. A state of catatonia is the ultimate extreme in psychotic symptomatology. This is the ego's final shut-down mechanism. The sufferer appears like a helpless child, locked in a basement. It is as if the ego has finally kidnapped him and cut him off from any interaction with reality. Again, much of the experience continues to mirror the mystical. The stillness and reduction in thought is the epitome of that which the spiritual adherent seeks, but ego and thinking mind are actually, even in this condition, still working hard to minimize any consequences of a still mind that may arise. That is why someone with poverty of thought has not so much experienced a cessation of thought, but rather thought has become slowed. This means that one thought might last many times longer than it normally would. So the few thoughts that remain are stretched across the patient's experience like duct tape, stopping the world beyond ego from coming in, thus enabling the thinking-ego paradigm to remain dominant.

Dominance is what ego strives to maintain at all costs and so, unless its potential dethronement has been reached via a patient and methodical process, it will react ferociously to every threat it is faced with. It will grow in size and complexity, but, paradoxically, reduce in organization, security and order with each hit. The more it struggles to keep itself intact, the less control it maintains. Ultimately, therefore, whichever way it goes, ego is still, in some way, headed towards the same destination. The journey of ego is fundamentally the journey of life – the journey of all our lives. For some, the pathway is more sweeping and dramatic than others, but there are mirrors between all our paths. And in the next chapter we will examine in more detail how it is that, one way or another, we are all treading the same circuit.

Chapter 10
The Wheel of Awakening

'Each man's life represents a road towards himself.'

Hermann Hesse

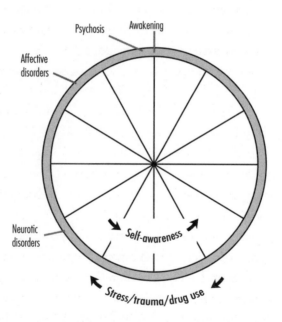

THIS DIAGRAM REPRESENTS what I call the wheel of awakening. It is an illustration of the psychological journey that I believe we are all on. It is the journey of ego. All of us are born at different places along the circle

– with different templates for ego already in place – and this is a consequence of whatever factors existed prior to our birth, for example, genetic inheritance or prenatal influences in the womb.

The forces of life then come into play. Trauma, stress and adverse life events tend to take us in a clockwise direction. The thinking mind leaps upon life's vicissitudes and adds layer upon layer to ego. And as new chapters are written into the story of our lives, the concept of 'me' gets heavier and heavier. This gradually makes us more vulnerable to further stressful and adverse experiences in life and ultimately it may push us into one of the neurotic disorders, whether that be generalized anxiety, phobias, panic attacks, or one of the more specific reactions like anorexia, obsessive compulsive disorder or PTSD. The exact nature of the disorder will, again, be a combination of our pre-existing vulnerabilities and the stress and traumas to which we were exposed.

At this point, it is worth remembering, and indeed elaborating upon, the caveat I issued in the introduction of this book. The ego can proliferate in a profusion of different ways depending on its starting point and the experiences to which it is exposed. There are as many different types of ego reaction, therefore, as there are egos. Pigeon-holing these reactions, at certain points along the cycle, as 'disorders' and subsequently labelling them with specific diagnoses is a simplification and therefore automatically inaccurate in every case. This inaccuracy risks becoming misleading, and even dangerous, if one's whole understanding of the experience ends at the level of diagnosis. This is why all psychiatric diagnoses, in my view, need to be taken with a heavy pinch of salt. They are perfect microcosmic examples of the limitations of our language-dominated thinking mind.

On the one hand, words help us communicate by describing things to each other, so they have a function – just as psychiatric terminology does. But, at the same time, they are inevitably an abbreviation of the thing they are describing – they are not the thing itself. The risk we introduce, when using words, therefore, is mistaking the label for the actual experience it is abbreviating. As pointed out in previous chapters, this is why the description or verbal recollection of certain events can trigger a reaction in our minds not dissimilar to that which would have occurred in the live event itself.

This risk is particularly acute in psychiatric diagnostic categories. The risk of seeing the label, not the person, is huge. In physical medicine, you could see hundreds of people with the same disorder and they would generally present along the same lines. Everyone who arrives in the emergency department with acute appendicitis, for example, is likely to have a similar range of symptoms. Not so in psychiatry. Though there are elements that may be similar in two presentations of, say, depression, the actual content of suffering – the issues they present with as their main concerns – will be very different in every case. That's why they're often so hard to detect. We try to fish out common themes to make a diagnosis, like changes in appetite, concentration, energy levels and sleep pattern, but the primary preoccupation of the patient will always vary; why they became depressed and what they find themselves ruminating upon will be different in every single case. This is something I find myself stressing to the junior doctors I train. If they describe a patient to me *purely* in terms of industry jargon – both diagnosis and symptoms – 'John is a paranoid schizophrenic who, upon relapse, becomes thought disordered and experiences auditory hallucinations' – I will usually stop them and ask them to describe what the actual experiences of the person concerned were, as opposed to what a chain of professionals labelled them to be.

Clearly diagnostic classification can inhibit our understanding of the patient's experience. A related, though even greater danger, however, is when a label starts actively to distort the experience we are observing. In my experience, most psychiatrists these days tend to agree that there is a swathe of people whom we see who don't really fit into any diagnostic category at all, yet clearly they are suffering quite acutely in a way that has brought them, often repeatedly, to the attention of psychiatric services. When discussing such cases we'll often explicitly acknowledge the difficulty in honestly fitting them into any diagnostic category and, therefore, how the diagnosis they have been given is more of a paper exercise to fulfil bureaucratic obligations than anything else. I will always tell my patients that there is an element of this in any diagnosis they are given and that what is more important – both for them and for me – is a fuller understanding of the experience they are going through.

Psychiatric diagnosis is, therefore, a severe example of the problem with words in general. It is a simplification that brings with it a series of inherent risks. But, at the same time, it is the only means we have at our disposal to communicate on certain levels. Just as we cannot have a dialogue without words, so we cannot have a discussion around the emotional pain and psychological suffering that are encountered in mental health settings without reference to the vocabulary of the day, namely that of 'illness' and 'disorder'. There are many debates on how to alter such definitions and I support any move that helps us improve the levels of accuracy and reduce any stigma that becomes attached to any labels we use, but I do so with the certainty that no description we deploy will ever be perfect. I always, therefore, counsel that any terminology used should be held very lightly. There are as many permutations of mental health or otherwise as there are people, and everyone's suffering is unique to them. The person who has the most right to define the experience is therefore the sufferer; sometimes an illness definition is preferred and sometimes it is not. Whenever the definition comes from the outside, however, a significant inaccuracy is always inbuilt.

This is one of the reasons why an individual's diagnosis will change so often. It is not at all uncommon for a patient's label to switch multiple times over their years in psychiatric treatment. And it is also why there are, not infrequently, disagreements between psychiatrists as to the diagnosis an individual has at any one point in time. Indeed, psychiatrists in different countries conceptualize the whole genre in very different ways. In the USA, for example, a number of psychiatrists believe that bipolar disorder can be diagnosed in an infant, whereas in the

UK, to my knowledge, that has never happened. The incidence of ADHD in children has also historically been much higher in America than in Europe. Another interesting perspective is the Scandinavian one where psychiatrists believe that diagnostic categories tend to fall into a hierarchy. In other words, they follow a pathway of severity from neurosis to affective disorders (depression and bipolar) all the way to psychosis. This has largely been my experience too. Though many people can travel directly into any one of the diagnoses we describe, most will travel from one to the other to the other. And this is, indeed, how I have represented it in the wheel as well.

Of course, continued travel in a clockwise direction from any point in the wheel is by no means inevitable. Usually further stress and obstacles in life will be involved in triggering each next stage. The arrows in the diagram, therefore, represent forces, while the specific points indicated on the wheel represent diagnoses, which must always be construed as guides and approximations, not realities in themselves. You will notice that the clockwise forces include drug use. Long-term, or even short-term, drug use can push those who are vulnerable toward mental illness and, again, this is something that every psychiatrist will be familiar with. Virtually every mental health unit contains a substantial proportion of people whose initiation or relapse into illnesses was triggered by drug use.

The effects of stimulant drugs have a lot of parallels with the paradoxical presentations of mental illness. On the one hand, a marked flare-up of ego is evoked; anything from mood swings to fear, paranoia and/

or hallucinations can occur. The ego starts to contort itself according to the environment around the user, trying hard to maintain its grip while, simultaneously, chinks of light start to creep in, allowing genuine mystical glimpses to take place. There are many reports of stimulant drug use producing flashes of insight akin to awakening and a report I read in Mark Epstein's book *Going on Being* brought this reality home to me. He talks about the experience of the well-known American spiritual teacher Ram Dass, and an Indian guru he once learnt from, by the name of Maharaj-ji. Having dabbled in drugs himself, Ram Dass recognized some parallel between awakening experiences and the experiences he had had on stimulants. He asked his guru about this and he replied by asking him to bring some to him so that he could experiment for himself and let him know. Somewhat taken aback, Ram Dass ultimately agreed and brought some LSD for his guru. The guru took several tablets. Nothing seemed to happen. He took a handful more and asked Ram Dass, 'Will it make me crazy?' A nervous Ram Dass replied 'Probably.' And so they waited. Still nothing. They waited throughout the day and night, and still nothing.

Epstein writes,

> Ram Dass was amazed at this display of psychic power. He knew from firsthand experience how the ego could be decimated by LSD. But here was a man who was unfazed by it. Maharaj-ji's ego was so flexible, so transparent, that the drug didn't seem to touch it.

The guru explained to Ram Dass that such drugs were known in India a long time ago, but knowledge about them was long since lost. While a form of awakening glimpse might occur it could never last, and so the experience ended up being as frustrating as it was pleasing: 'Once you get the message, you have to hang up the phone.' This, coupled with the risk of provoking serious mental ill health, is why virtually no spiritual teacher recommends such methods.

Of course, such drugs are more often used as a form of recreation or, more likely, anaesthesia. They are used as a temporary escape hatch from the suffering of life but, while the transient feeling may lift the burden for moments, beneath the surface the weight of ego continues to build, taking the sufferer further and further in a clockwise direction along the wheel depicted above.

Parallel with the different categories of mental illness, there are also what psychiatrists refer to as personality disorders. These often coexist with various mental disorders and they essentially represent another per-mutation of ego expansion. In this case, however, they are reactions that set in early in life – often as a result of abuse, faulty learning or neglect in childhood – and, consequently, the ego proliferation is channelled less into circumscribed symptoms of mental illness, and more into generalized character traits. Prominent forms include antisocial (psychopathic) personality disorder, where there appears to be a lack of empathy for others or remorse for transgression, and narcissistic personality disorder, which is characterized by grandiosity and an overwhelming need for the admiration of others. More common still are the emotionally unstable personality disorders, like borderline personality disorder, which involves a lack of ability to regulate emotions, explosive behaviours and sometimes self-harm. Problems, in all cases, centre around difficulty in adhering to societal norms, with often serious deficits in the ability to form and maintain interpersonal relationships.

With their burgeoning egos, people with personality disorders are more vulnerable to the development of mental illness, and at the same time, the heavier ego gets, the more cracks it simultaneously develops as a result.

This is also why, the further up the wheel – in a clock-wise direction – we go, the more profound the flashes of insight seem to be. A few of those who suffer neurotic disorders may experience forms of depersonalization; a few more of those with depression may experience some personal and spiritual growth as a result of working through the experience and, more commonly still, those with bipolar disorder may experience strong spiritual themes in relation to the core symptoms themselves. Indeed, the higher one gets in the wheel, the more spiritually laced the symptoms become, and so the more mystical the experience of mental illness starts to sound. This also explains why there are such strong parallels between the experience of psychosis and that of mystical awakening. It is almost as if the ego is cannibalizing itself from the inside out.

Ego rises like a soufflé, only to start springing leaks as a result. Like a sinking ship disappearing into the sea, the process is a chaotic one and manifests differently in each person. To the outside observer it may appear as if there is a battle going on between ego and that which lies beyond it, and I must admit that it feels like that sometimes with my patients. But, in fact, it is really ego just fighting with itself. That which lies beyond it, just is; it is stillness, emptiness, everything and nothing. It doesn't have to fight with ego because, fundamentally, it is not separate from ego. It is just ego that thinks it is separate from everything else.

This is also why, when trying to understand these phenomena, it is important to keep reminding ourselves that language – itself a tool of ego – is always going to leave us with an incomplete picture. It is not possible for me to talk about ego, without doing so as if it is a separate entity, and that is because I am using language to do so. That is one of the limitations of this model, or indeed any 'model' at all. So while, on the one hand, I talk about a separate ego, it can also be argued that it is essentially arbitrary to distinguish between an 'ego' and the forces that act upon it. In reality, as many wise mental health professionals will attest, the issues we are talking about are actually whole system issues and not just issues of an individual. The so called 'disorder' is actually a collaborative experience that develops from and affects a whole family, society and even culture. The forces that I describe as 'acting upon' the concept of 'ego' are thus, in many ways, not really separable from the ego itself. Without your experiences and environment, you could not be you.

This becomes particularly important when we start to consider treatment, because it means that we need to direct our intervention towards the whole environment, as well as the individual, and I will address this in a subsequent chapter on psychiatric treatment. In that section of the book, I will also argue that there is a need to go deeper than current notions of 'treatment' alone, and move beyond it to the profound personal work of growth and development, which is represented in the anticlockwise direction on the wheel.

Unlike the rapid, jerky clockwise forces of trauma, abuse and drugs, this anticlockwise motion depicts the slow and gradual force of self-awareness, all the way up to awakening. Where the clockwise current requires little or no free will to follow it, the anticlockwise current represents patient and deliberate effort on the part of the individual. It is not a fast or violent force, but a slow and steady one. In this direction, rather than building up, ego is slowly fading away.

The anticlockwise journey is both a psychological and a spiritual one and it has been known, in various guises, since the dawn of time. From the Buddha to Jesus to Freud, they were all, in one way or another, describing paths that take the traveller in this direction. Above the doorway of the Temple of Delphi, where the famed Oracle sat in ancient times and held audiences with princes and emperors from around the world, there was a sign 'Know Thyself'. That, quite simply, is the purpose of life. And somewhere, deep inside each of us, we have always known this.

Though buried under multiple layers of inflamed ego, this reality is also keenly felt by sufferers of mental illness too. The chinks of light that their illness affords them are also its gifts, and this brings about a wisdom, a deeper sense of knowing that clinicians with a higher level of self-awareness themselves will tend to recognize. In some ways it will feel like looking in a mirror, the same image but reversed. They are looking across at each other from opposite ends of the wheel but often, at the same time, also travelling closer and closer to one other as they reach the top.

For me, a significant proof of this is the phenomenon of autism. On the one hand, sufferers of autism experience a number of difficulties in social communication, both verbal and non-verbal. As a result, they often spend time alone and can have real difficulty when it comes to being amongst groups of people or in environments or routines that are not familiar to them, and this may occasionally result in eruptions of anger or even violence. On one level, therefore, it might seem that they have a significant shell around them, like a dense ego that is shielding them from contact with the outside world. But, in fact, if one explores the phenomenon more deeply, many with autistic spectrum disorders describe a simultaneous heightened awareness of the environment around them. Sufferers will often describe an almost overwhelming sensitivity to the senses of sight, smell, taste, touch or hearing, not unlike the increased sensitivity we are trained to develop through mindfulness practice. And so, in many ways, they are both more open to the world around them and more closed off from it at the same time.

The writer William Stillman has autism and, through his own quest to understand himself, he has undergone a journey of great courage and spiritual growth. In recent years he has met, interviewed and helped many people with autism and their families and he has written prolifically on the subject. In one of his books he details the numerous stories he has heard over the years and how 'their anecdotes underscored the heightened awareness, innate gentleness and exquisite sensitivity in a number of people with autism; that is the capacity to perceive all things seen and unseen'. This is something he is witness to in himself from an early age.

In fact, just as I did in earlier chapters of this book, he too has identified ways in which a number of symptoms of autism seem to mirror practices designed to enhance spiritual awareness, such as the repetition of mundane activities. Such 'repetitive movement [is] not unlike the constant rocking, hand-flapping, or twirling of some individuals with autism!'

This is why, despite their social deficits, so many around autistic people describe them as 'gifted' and notice their ability to make connections and see more of the world than many of the rest of us. People with autism often pay a heavy price for this, however, as there is an increased vulnerability to mental illness that comes along with it. Again, the heaving, cracking ego flares up from time to time like an unstable volcano spewing its lava into the air. But even throughout such episodes – whether they be of depression, bipolar or psychosis – the parallels with the experiences of the spiritual seeker are unmistakable.

The main difference between them appears to be one of volition but it is worth noting that not even this is entirely clear cut. On the one hand, the anticlockwise journey tends to be a product of deliberate effort, as we have discussed, while the clockwise journey tends to be the result of the circumstances of life and/or inheritance. But it is also possible for everyone voluntarily to journey in the clockwise direction as well. In other words, it is possible to approach awakening willingly through the path of ego proliferation, rather than gradual dissolution. Why would one choose to do this, you might ask? Well, it is because, in such cases, one is effectively carrying the ego along for the ride, as it were, which means that all the awakening glimpses that are experienced will appear to be of a more tangible nature – that is interpreted through a significant ego prism – thus facilitating unique forms of wisdom and relatable insights. This is the path of the shaman.

Many writers on the subject describe how shamanism has existed for over 10,000 years in just about every ancient civilization known to man and taking such a journey into the depths of one's psyche has been a time-honoured passage for every would-be shaman. Clearly, however, it is a path of grave danger that requires long training and, even then, will sometimes cause the individual to slip in and out of mental illness. Indeed a volitional component can exist for many people who experience mental illness. I have known many patients who originally experienced their symptoms as a result of abuse or drugs, who then started knowingly engaging in actions – such as deprivation-based stress, repetitive behaviours or even drug taking – in order to induce their symptoms later on. And with that then comes both the wisdom and the escape, and the danger too.

Whichever route is taken, however, the point of awakening can be a common destination for all, but its consequences can be as different as night and day. The actual moment of awakening can be an entirely different experience depending on the direction and intention via which it is reached, and we will explore this further in the next chapter.

Chapter 11
Ego Dissolution

'The secret of life is to die before you die,
and find that there is no death.'

Eckhart Tolle

EVERY AWAKENING IS A FORM of death. What kind of death, depends on the route via which the awakening was attained. The deliberate and effortful work of self-awareness ultimately leads to a death of the ego perspective: the death of everything you thought you were up to that point. Suddenly you can see beyond the narrow lens of ego and the illusory nature of separation becomes clear. It is not something that can be described, drawn or known in the intellectual sense, but it can be experienced in the truest and fullest sense of the word. From that point forward you realize that you are not really the 'me' that you thought you were. You realize that this idea of 'I' was just a peep-hole through which you viewed the world and now, through the process of self awareness, you have become aware of what is around it, and indeed aware of the peep-hole itself – the ego. You can look at it, you can feel it, you can sense it. And it's not you. The ego is a part of you, but it is not the totality of who you are.

Of course, so long as ego exists – and it will, as long as we have a body – the perspective will be there for us to use, but not to be used by. It's gravitational pull will continue to exert pressure on us, however, and occasional, sometimes regular, lapses into the ego channel will occur. The difference, this time, is that you will know it, and that's why it can hurt more than it ever used to. I often find myself lapsing into selfishness and judgement but now it comes with an inner pain and from that stems a determination to learn from each lapse.

Again, the experience is well documented in Adyashanti's brilliant book *End of Your World*:

> It's only at this particular point that people start to realize that almost everything that previously motivated them in life was self-centred. I do not mean that in a negative or judgemental way; I simply mean that the driving force propelling us through life when we are in the dream state is very self-centred . . . The dream state is the state where we perceive separation, where we think we are a separate entity and a separate being. That separate being is always seeking something – love, approval, success, money, maybe even enlightenment. But with real awakening, that whole structure begins to dissolve under one's feet . . . There is still a human being there; we don't disappear into a puff of smoke. Even our personality remains intact . . .
>
> The difference is that once we have seen beyond the veil of separation, *identification* with our particular personality begins to dissolve.

But he's clear that it's not all plain sailing from there:

> The ego may resist this dissolution with every-
> thing it has. It may bring out the entirety of its
> arsenal . . . The dream state has a gravitational
> force; it has a tendency to pull consciousness into
> itself . . . This gives rise to what I call the 'I got it,
> I lost it phenomenon' . . . This 'I got it, I lost it'
> phenomenon is the struggle, as it were, between
> our true nature and our imagined sense of self
> . . . [this] vacillation can be very painful. In fact,
> it is much more painful to act in a way that we
> know is not true once we've seen that it is not
> true.

So, in order to maintain and deepen awakening, the
work of self-awareness needs to continue. We are back on
the wheel but it is almost as if we have been born again
to resume our journey from a new point somewhere in
a less ego-dominated part of the circle. This will occur
however we reach ego-dissolution, but if we arrive at it
via a clockwise direction – say, via psychosis or drug use
(and if we managed to survive that) – then considerable
work will still need to be done. In such cases, after a
degree of ego-shedding, one is still likely to reappear in
the circle at a relatively ego-heavy place and so a lot of
ongoing effort will be required to work towards a more
lasting reawakening via an anticlockwise route.

Whichever way we get there, however, the objective
will be to continue returning to awakening again and
again, so that our ego continues to thin and, thus, serve
us more and rule us less. The more we go through this

process, the more we find that paradoxical things start to happen as a result: our attachment to the world reduces, but our passion for it increases. Language and logic hold less and less value, while, at the same time, our ability to wield them keeps growing. Our very sense of life and death starts to alter – as we know that we have an existence beyond this pure 'me' that we thought we were – but our love of life and compassion for all living things only strengthens with it. Awakening brings death closer, the notion, feeling and sense of death, but it is no longer so much of a terror to be feared, hidden and suppressed at all costs.

There is, therefore, a close connection between the point of awakening and the point of death. When ego-dissolution has been arrived at gradually, it becomes a rebirth, but when arrived at abruptly, it can be brought about through physical death. When an individual is too fused to ego, dissolution of ego will also mean death of the physical body – through suicide or other chaotic means. It is as if the ego would rather extinguish the organism than allow its liberation.

So a planned awakening can occur before physical death, but an unplanned one often only occurs at the point of death. That is why awakening experiences are sometimes referred to as 'dying before you die'. It is also why an experience akin to awakening is sometimes what occurs at the moment of death, as reported by survivors of near-death experiences. In a landmark book on the subject, Dutch cardiologist Dr Pim Van Lommel describes an experience in 1969, early in his cardiology training. He and his team successfully resuscitated a man who had suffered a cardiac arrest and had been clinically dead for over four minutes. Everyone was pleased with the outcome, except the patient himself. He was extremely emotional and sad to have been yanked back from an experience he instantly described, which he said was almost too powerful for words, involving light, colours and a tunnel. But this could not be, thought Dr Van Lommel. There was no consciousness in that period so where did the memory the man was describing come from? He was clinically dead for a number of minutes. There was no oxygen going to the brain so there was no way in which current medical knowledge could explain the experience he was having.

This troubled the doctor as he rose through the ranks over the years that followed, so much so that in the mid-eighties he decided to conduct a scientific study on the subject, interviewing a cohort of his patients who had survived cardiac arrests. He asked them if they had any recollection of their period of clinical death and he was rocked by the discovery that 24% of them actually described similar near-death experiences (NDEs). He then did a wider study of 344 patients and, again, discovered that 62 patients (18%) reported an NDE.

Van Lommel catalogued the various descriptions he was given and detailed the core themes that seemed to underpin most experiences. Many had overwhelming feelings of peace, joy and bliss, and an intensity that drove the experience beyond the level of anything they had encountered before, indeed, beyond words altogether. This ineffability runs through many of the first-person testimonies reported in his book. Here is an example:

> I was there . . . It's simply too much for human
> words . . . where there's no distinction between
> good and evil, and time and place don't exist.
> And an immense, intense pure love compared to
> which love in our human dimension pales into
> insignificance . . . where there's no distinction
> between life and death.

After trawling all the research literature, Van Lommel
found that the experience was, in fact, uniformly
common around the globe with 600,000 reported
NDE cases in the Netherlands, 2 million in the United
Kingdom and more than 9 million in the United States.
This is despite the fact that NDEs are thought to be
grossly under-reported in hospitals because patients may
fear evoking a negative reaction or even a psychiatric
diagnosis from the clinicians in charge of their care at
the time.

Indeed, I have heard of such episodes within my own
circle of friends. One occurred several decades ago to
someone known as Julian Skinner. Every year his family
would visit some of the lovely secluded beaches along
the south coast of Cornwall. Whenever he was there,
he would while away the hours paddling in the shallow
water along the seashore. One summer, at the age of
seven, while he was enjoying a refreshing meander
through the gentle ripples, a violent undercurrent
suddenly started to suck him out to sea. The tide
immersed him completely. He managed to leap upward
to grab a gasp of breath before the current dragged him
inexorably outwards and deeper into the water. This

time he wasn't able to get back up. His life started to drain away. At this tender age he felt his final moments upon him. Then something profound seemed to come over him: 'I can't really describe it,' he says, when he talks about it today. Words just aren't applicable, yet it felt like the first truly authentic experience of his life. 'It was a deep sense of acceptance. And all I can really call it is love.' Yet, in many ways, it was much more than even that word suggests. Despite its indescribability, what he learnt unmistakably at that moment, even at this delicate age, was that death was not the end of life.

Countless such episodes have been collated over the years and research into near-death experiences has come a long way; there is now an International Association for Near-Death Studies. Its chair, Professor Janet Holden, describes NDEs as 'reported memories of extreme psychological experiences with frequent "paranormal", transcendental and mystical elements, which occur during a special state of consciousness arising during a period of real or imminent physical, psychological, emotional or spiritual death, and these experiences are followed by common after effects.'

Of note here is the way in which a near-death experience is defined as an event that can occur at the moment of physical death, or at the moment of a different kind of 'psychological, emotional or spiritual death'. And these psychologically derived or physically derived phenomena both show 'common after effects'. Indeed, those who survive NDEs describe the manifestations of authentic ego-dissolution in their day-to-day life thereafter. Here's a typical example from Van Lommel's cases:

I'm no longer afraid of death because I'll never forget what happened to me there. Now I'm certain that life goes on. Over the years I've undergone a number of changes. I feel a strong connection with nature ... I've become more patient and peaceful. I can see things in perspective now.

The effect was also truly profound for Julian Skinner. His life was ultimately saved, but the experience stayed with him for the rest of it. And, though, as he entered adulthood, he got dragged by the ubiquitous currents of convention into a successful professional life in the pharmaceutical industry, the memory remained a searing one. Then one day, he could resist the yearning no longer, a yearning that was ignited all those years ago in a small beach in Cornwall. He took the bold move to abandon his career and enter a spiritual search, which ultimately took him to a Zen monastery in Japan where he became a monk. Fifteen years later, Julian became the first Englishman to become a fully ordained Zen master in the Rinzai tradition. He was promoted to vice-abbot of his temple but instead of taking over the temple when the old abbot retired, he decided to return to the UK in 2007 to serve in his homeland. He is now known by his students – among whom I count myself – as Daizan Roshi. He has a *dojo* in South London, called Zenways, and shares his experiences and teachings with hundreds of people around the UK and Europe. He has become a deeply inspirational figure for all of us, and he is someone who I am truly honoured to call a friend.

So the dissolution of ego, and the awakening that results, can occur both at the moment of psychological death or the moment of physical death. And for those who are headed to this moment of awakening through more rapid and violent means, the latter becomes a real possibility. This applies just as much to those who have arrived at this point via the physically violent pathway of cardiac arrest, as it does to those who have arrived via the egoically violent pathway of mental illness and distress.

And herein lies the greatest tragedy of mental illness. The ego has the ability, *in extremis*, to take you down with it. The relentless torment of an out-of-control ego can lead the sufferer to conclude that there is only one way out. The mother of a suicide victim who had suffered severe depression once said to me that, even though he took his own life, she saw him very much as a victim: 'It was basically a take-over job.' To me, that's a very good way of describing what really happened to her son. The thinking mind went into overdrive and hijacked the sufferer to the illusory point of no return, where self-destruction seemed like the only option.

There are over 4,000 suicide deaths every year in the UK. Suicide is the tenth leading cause of death in the USA, and the third leading cause of death for people between the ages of 10 and 24. And the potential is far greater than even that. An estimated 11 attempted suicides occur for every suicide death. Most suicides are, of course, a product of mental illness, and it has been found in a variety of studies that the mortality rate for the seriously mentally ill is more than twice the mortality rate for a comparable general population. In fact, the only cause of death that shows a greater mortality rate in the general population is cancer.

Thankfully, of course, the vast majority of people who experience mental illness will never get to this point. The advance of many will stall at some point in the circle, and others will be able to turn their trajectory around altogether, but by examining suicide we gain a window into the machinations of the mind in its most extreme state. Suicide is a case of the mind hijacking the body. And the mind, with its prime creation of ego, is an endlessly vacillating entity, oscillating and gyrating in every direction until its last moment. In the UK, the detoxification of the domestic gas supply caused a significant drop in the suicide rate. The reason for this was that, up to that point, one of the most common methods for suicide was putting one's head in the oven and turning it on. Once the gas supply was detoxified, that was no longer an option. In order to die in a non-violent way, the suicidal person would have to try the next best thing, which would mean a walk across the street to a chemist to buy some tablets and, perhaps with some additional alcohol, take an overdose. But the introduction of these small, easily surmountable obstacles was enough to stop swathes of people from actually going through with it. This taught us that suicide is never a done deal till the moment it happens. It is a constant 'yes I will, no I won't' oscillation, and if you interrupt the process in time, the whole act may ultimately be prevented.

This one statistic provides us with a glimpse into the

chaos that grips the suicidal mind. And with even a small degree of self-awareness we can recognize it as no more than an exaggerated version of the oscillations that go on within all our own minds all the time. That's why mental illness scares us so much: we can all sense, at some level, that none of us is more than a couple of steps away from even its most extreme manifestations. This societal fear has historically filtered through to treatment itself. Sprawling asylums and barbaric methods such as frontal lobotomy and insulin coma therapy were all manifestations of this fear. And even today no treatment system is immune from this desire to suppress that which we refuse to recognize as a variant of our own inner nature. It is a kind of manifestation, on a societal scale, of ego fighting itself.

The solution, therefore, must at least in part include a pathway out of attachment to ego itself. The irony, of course, is that precisely such a pathway often presents itself to the sufferer as the hyperactive ego starts to fracture. The key to a more robust treatment – in addition to many conventional methods, where needed – is thus to harness this very energy that they are encountering, even in the throes of this most profound inner turmoil. It is my belief that those who have experienced mental illness are actually primed for awakening. Many will have a heightened receptivity to the self-awareness work that will take them in the opposite direction, towards a safer and more durable awakening, should they choose to embark upon such a path. With this as a new goal for treatment, I believe that many more people can be healed and indeed transformed than is currently the case, and in the final part of this book, I will explore how this might come to pass.

PART FOUR

Treatment and Transformation

Healing through Wholeness

Chapter 12

Psychiatric Treatment

'The mind is its own place, and in itself can make a heaven of hell, a hell of heaven.'

John Milton

A MAJOR SHIFT IN THE WAY emotional and mental turmoil was viewed in the West occurred around the time of the Enlightenment. Prior to this, such experiences were understood through the prism of literal religious interpretation, in which spirit or Satanic forces were deemed to be responsible. This applied as much to epilepsy and other neurological ailments as it did to purely mental experiences. In the eighteenth century, however, physicians started toying with the idea that such maladies had a physical cause. It was the physician Thomas Willis who, in the seventeenth century, coined the term 'neurology', and he started to locate certain mental functions to particular regions of the brain. Later physicians then followed his lead, developing further explanations to describe emotional dysfunctions in organic terms. Herman Boerhaave, an influential professor at the University of Leiden in Germany, systematically catalogued every form of mental illness as a bodily disorder. Melancholy, for example, was due, in his description, to a 'dissipation' (evaporation) of the most volatile elements of the blood and thickening of the 'black, fat, earthy residue' that it left behind, resulting in lethargy. Another professor of medicine, Friedrich Hoffmann, attributed all psychopathology to various vessels, fibres and pores, and Scot George Cheyne attributed disorders of thought and mood-swings to defects of the digestive and nervous systems, which led to slackness, excessive tension and obstruction. It was Nicholas Robinson, however, who firmly embedded this line of reasoning into the Newtonian physical world paradigm, when he stated in his 1729 book *A New System of the Spleen* that, 'Every change of the mind indicates a change in the bodily organs,' because he was certain that insanity was based on 'real mechanical afflictions of body and motion'.

Thus was launched a new paradigm in which mental and emotional problems were seen as essentially extensions of disorders of the physical body. The Philadelphia physician Benjamin Rush, who is officially recognized by the American Psychiatric Association as the 'father of modern psychiatry', held that all mental illnesses were the result, in some form or other, of damaged or impaired blood and, as a result, the prescribed cure was bloodletting.

A major validation for the notion that physical changes were the fundamental root of mental disorders followed soon after when, in 1822, Antoine Laurent Bayle described General Paresis of the Insane (GPI). This was a disorder that involved escalating levels of mental disturbance from personality changes at the beginning, all the way through to grandiose and paranoid delusions before, ultimately, death. Today we know these as the symptoms of advanced (tertiary) syphilis, and although at the time Bayle did not have knowledge of the micro-organisms involved, he was still able to correlate these symptoms with the very marked changes observed in the brain during autopsies of the deceased. This was one of the first clues, therefore, that brain changes could be directly observed in people suffering a form of mental disorder.

Findings such as these gave the famous French physician Jean-Martin Charcot – Clinical Professor of the Nervous System at the Salpetrière hospital in Paris – the conviction that sufficient detailed observation of all symptoms of mental ailment would ultimately unearth the physical process underpinning them. 'These diseases', he stated, 'do not form, in pathology, a class apart, governed by other physiological laws than the common ones.' He spent time particularly researching hysteria which he believed had a set of underlying organic causes waiting to be discovered, just like any other physical disorder.

The materialist movement in mental health took a particularly ugly turn in the early nineteenth century with the advent of phrenology, articulated by Franz Joseph Gall. In it, he maintained that the size of an individual's brain governed the power of its operation, and that different elements of its shapes and contours – as reflected in the shape of the skull – correlated with personality types. Although this overarching theory was ultimately discredited after its adoption by the far right and ultimately Nazi Germany, it was, nevertheless, another stepping stone on the pathway to the total physicalization of mental illness. As Roy Porter – Professor of the Social History of Medicine at University College, London – put it, in his book *Madness: A Brief History*,

> Phrenology or not . . . the idea of a physical sub-strate of insanity buttressed the doctors' claim that psychiatric practice should be exclusive to the medically qualified, sanctioned laboratory research and gave credibility to the ragbag of physical treatments, notably sedatives, bathing, purging, and bleeding, which formed the stock-in-trade of the profession.

A landmark in the materialist march within psychiatry came about in the form of a seminal textbook by German professor Wilhelm Griesinger entitled *Pathology and Therapy of Psychiatric Disorders*, in which he declared that 'Mental illnesses are brain diseases . . . Every mental illness is rooted in brain disease.' For him it was crucial that psychiatry ally itself with general medicine and that all such patients be investigated, diagnosed and treated in a scientific way, just as any patient with any physical disorder would be.

An examination of the 'scientific treatments' that flowed from this philosophy, however, reveals what would be considered today as little more than a thinly disguised form of brutality. By the twentieth century, for example, surgical methods had been discovered to 'treat' these unwanted experiences. The frontal lobotomy involved severing all connections between the prefrontal cortex – a large section of the frontal lobe, behind the forehead – and the rest of the brain. This is the part of the brain that had now been implicated in cognitive, emotional and social behaviour and personality in general. The lobotomy was believed to be a cure for everything from panic disorder and depression to mania and schizophrenia. The procedure was highly invasive and involved drilling holes in the scalp. It therefore required significant amounts of time in the operating theatre and had to be performed by trained neurosurgeons. This limited its availability and so kept down the number of people who could undergo the procedure.

In 1945, however, an American psychiatrist by the name of Walter Freeman came up with a way round this problem. He took an ice-pick from his kitchen and started testing the idea of a 'trans-orbital' lobotomy. This involved lifting the upper eyelid and going in just between the top of the eye and the edge of the eye socket. He made the procedure so simple that it could now be performed in psychiatric clinics without need for an operating theatre. The lobotomy was unleashed. Freeman charged just $25 for each procedure, and he personally performed an estimated 3,400 lobotomies over the next four decades. All around him a wave caught on. In 1949 5,074 procedures were undertaken in the USA alone, and by 1951 over 18,608 individuals had been lobotomized. The number of people left permanently incapacitated by the procedure, however, steadily mounted. In 1950, the USSR banned it, with doctors claiming that 'it turned an insane person into an idiot', and over in America high-profile cases such as Rosemary Kennedy – sister of President John F Kennedy – who was left severely disabled by the procedure, began to turn the tide against it, ushering its demise over the following years.

Before the Second World War chemical methods of suppressing the mentally ill also started coming to the fore with the invention of Insulin Coma Therapy. This involved repeatedly injecting patients with large doses of insulin in order to produce daily comas over several weeks. The daily insulin dose was gradually increased to 100–150 units until comas were induced. Occasionally doses of up to 450 units were used. This carried on until the patient was put through about 50 or 60 comas.

In 1953 British psychiatrist Harold Bourne published a paper entitled 'The insulin myth' in the *Lancet*, in which he argued that there was no real evidence to support the use of insulin coma therapy and several randomized controlled trials a couple of years later demonstrated that this was indeed the case. Their use fell out of favour soon after.

Methodologies such as double-blind randomized controlled trials became more commonplace in the continuing search for physical treatments. These studies are designed in a particularly rigorous empirical way, in that a group of patients taking the new drug is compared to a group of patients taking a chemically inert tablet that has no biological effect (a placebo), and neither the patient nor the doctor knows who is in which group – hence double-blind – as they are randomly assigned by an unconnected third party at the start of the trial. A comparison in symptom change over time between the two groups enables one to determine whether or not the intended drug actually has the desired effect.

In the 1950s several large-scale trials were launched to investigate the particular antipsychotic effects of a drug known as chlorpromazine. It was initially used on psychiatric patients because of its powerful calming effect; however, over time, clinicians began to notice some potentially beneficial specific effects on the symptoms of psychosis itself. The first clinical trials were conducted in France on 38 patients with psychosis and the results showed a significant reduction in delusions and hallucination for many of the patients. A further study in Montreal on 70 patients produced similar findings. The first large-scale randomized controlled trials took place in the 1960s and they seemed to corroborate this effect.

The sedating effect remained a problem, however, and a number of researchers started looking for ways to minimize this with other more stimulating drugs. It was through this process that the first antidepressant, imipramine, came to be discovered. In the initial trials, symptoms such as hopelessness, despair and depressive apathy appeared to improve in a significant proportion of patients. Larger-scale trials again seemed to confirm this.

Like chlorpromazine, however, it too had a number of unpleasant side effects and so its use remained at a fairly low level. Gradually, newer-generation drugs – both antidepressants and antipsychotics – were developed and, at time of release, all were billed as having successively improved side-effect profiles. However, over time, it became increasingly apparent that each of these second- and third-generation drugs had a range of significantly disturbing side effects of their own. Many second-generation antipsychotic drugs increase the risk of developing diabetes, and several of the newer antidepressants produce weight gain, as well as risks of increased anxiety and agitation, and, additionally, a number of potentially dangerous cardiac side effects. This picture is also echoed with mood-stabilizing drugs like lithium which carry significant risk of impairing kidney function, while others can be problematic for the liver.

For most psychiatrists today, therefore, psychiatric treatment is a delicate balancing game; weighing the costs and benefits of the interventions available. There is no doubt that many of the drugs we prescribe produce genuine symptom reduction but, at the same time, they usually also come with a significant physical health price. Many psychiatrists – though by no means all – will tend to err on the side of caution and prescribe the lowest dose possible for these reasons. An additional concern, however, and one that goes all the way back to the data from the original studies is that – for antipsychotics, antidepressants and mood-stabilizers – far too many patients seem to relapse while still on the medication. Again, this is a common experience for psychiatrists everywhere. The same faces keep re-presenting year after year and, sometimes, numerous times within the same year. A proportion of this is clearly the result of poor compliance with medication, but often relapse occurs even after the medication is taken exactly as prescribed.

The data on this are laid out clearly in one of the standard textbooks of postgraduate psychiatry, *Companion to Psychiatric Studies*, by Johnson, Freeman and Zealley. This describes a well-known longitudinal study, for example, in which patients on antipsychotics were followed up for two years, and it was found that 48% relapsed. Antipsychotics are also available in long-acting injectable (depot) form and this means that the clinical team can know exactly when the medication is being received. Studies then examined how the relapse rate in people on depot compared to oral medication yet they found, even in this group, 'the 2 year relapse rate remained substantial'. In fact, 'There was no difference between the two groups.' And the outcomes are no better where treatments for mood disorders are concerned either. 'Patients have a high certainty of short term recovery but the near certainty of subsequent recurrence with or without treatment.'

The most significant blow to pharmacological therapies, however, came about towards the end of the millennium when Professor Irving Kirsch – currently lecturer in medicine at Harvard Medical School – did what is known as a meta-analysis, compiling all the data from the main published randomized controlled trials for antidepressants. He, indeed, found a clinically significant effect for these drugs but, when he looked at the control-group responses to the placebos, he actually found that they had improved about 75% as much as those on the antidepressant. The placebo effect was enormous. 'We wondered, what's going on?' recalls Kirsch. The next thing he did was to ask the US Food and Drug Administration for data on the trials that drug companies such as Eli Lilley carried out on their antidepressants during development but did not go on to publish. They were legally obliged, under the US Freedom of Information Act, to provide these details, and when Kirsch put all the data together he found that, in fact, there was even less difference between the improvements produced by Prozac – and several other antidepressant drugs – and placebo. In fact, it was now evident that 82% of their effects were no different to placebo. In other words, the biggest single reason that people were responding to antidepressants was what we call 'the placebo effect'.

But what is the placebo effect and how does it chime with our understanding of the brain? All of pharmacology is based on the notion that a drug has a specific effect on brain chemistry, and it is this effect that then produces the changes in symptoms. But if a belief that a pill will work – regardless of what that pill actually does – itself has an impact on symptoms, then clearly there must be a level, beyond the physical level of the brain, that is having an effect. According to the materialist view of science, this should not happen. In 2005, *New Scientist* published a paper entitled '13 Things That Don't Make Sense'. In it was listed a series of uncontestable findings that are considered wholly anomalous from the scientific standpoint. Number one on this list was the placebo effect.

Former Cambridge biologist Rupert Sheldrake articulates well the problem it poses for the scientific community:

> If materialism were an adequate foundation for
> medicine, placebo responses ought not to occur
> . . . Placebo responses show that health and sick-
> ness are not just a matter of physics and chem-
> istry. They also depend on hopes, meanings and
> beliefs. Placebo responses are an integral part of
> healing.

A number of psychiatrists have pointed out that the
placebo effect in psychiatric drugs may actually run
deeper than even Kirsch first thought. This is because
some of the intense and immediate side effects that
many of these drugs produce, for example nightmares,
sedation, stiffness and restless legs, can lead a subject in
a clinical trial to realize pretty quickly whether or not
he is taking the active substance or just a placebo. In a
trial this is called 'breaking the blind': the clinician or
patient or both have worked out for themselves which
tablet they were actually taking. In such cases, a trial that
was considered to be 'double blind' wasn't so at all. This
suggests that the results that pointed to higher efficacy
levels for the drug in question, over and above those of
a placebo, are not in fact as robust as was first thought.

Biological psychiatry started as a series of firm convictions before there was no more than a limited base of
evidence for it. The idea that disorders of the mind are
all the product of solid, tangible, physical dysfunctions
of the brain gained currency across the scientific
community so rapidly that the medical profession found
itself embarking upon a series of frenzied leaps from one
(often barbaric) physical treatment to another, before

finally giving birth to the age of psychopharmacology. Current pharmacological treatments certainly come with more evidence of benefit than a lot of their predecessors, but the case for them is by no means airtight. While no one can doubt the relief they have brought to countless sufferers of mental ill health across a variety of conditions over the last half century, there remains a large deficit in the ability of mainstream academia to explain exactly how or why they work. A number of hypotheses exist, but none of them explain the story as fully as the treatments for most physical disorders, such as, say, the action of antibiotics on infectious diseases. And, of course, where they do work in the short term, relapses keep occurring in the long term. Indeed, the number of people experiencing mental illness around the world is no less today than it was fifty years ago. In fact, a number of indicators, such as claims for sickness/ disability benefit, suggest it might be increasing.

In my experience, many psychiatrists are becoming increasingly uncomfortable with this brick wall that biological psychiatry seems to have hit. They sense that, for all the benefit it has brought, it is seriously missing something from the bigger picture. Twenty-nine such concerned psychiatrists wrote a special article in the December 2012 edition of the *British Journal of Psychiatry* – the in-house magazine of the Royal College of Psychiatrists – entitled 'Psychiatry Beyond the Current Paradigm'. In it they asserted that, to them,

> Psychiatry is not neurology; it is not a medicine of the brain. Although mental health problems

undoubtedly have a biological dimension, in
their very nature they reach beyond the brain to
involve social, cultural and psychological dimensions. These cannot always be grasped through
. . . biomedicine.

Most now recognize, as I outlined in Chapter 10, that
the 'syndrome' or issue that needs addressing is as much
an interpersonal and social one as it is an internal or
physical one, and this is why interventions that involve
families and social networks are often the most effective
in the long term. Mental illness, in my experience, is
usually the result of a collection of egos, not just one, in
an interplay with each other – as suggested in the wheel
of awakening, even though it might ultimately manifest
in the mind of a single individual. This means that an
effective treatment approach needs to involve a whole
social network working together on their egos, and this
includes the professionals as well. That is also why, if
truly embraced, such methodologies become genuine
growth experiences, not just for the patient, but for
family, friends and clinicians too.

Finland was one of the first countries to pioneer
such an approach and they termed it 'Open Dialogue'.
Treating acutely unwell patients involves regular 'network meetings' between the patient, her wider network
of family and friends and the clinical team as well. The
meetings are open, non-hierarchical and democratic,
and the issue is approached, not from the perspective
of 'professionals' here to help 'patients', but of people
coming together to find mutual solutions for the

problems at hand, using the resources available to them. This also means that they start out embracing the uncertainty of the moment and working out a pathway through a genuine process of listening without templates and pre-conceived notions. Sometimes this may result in medication and/or hospitalization (even in secure hospitals, which still exist in the region), but more often it will manage to avoid these things and help the patients find meaning through their experience, in a collaborative process with friends, family and carers, and grow through it together and organically. This can work for any disorder, even psychosis; in fact some of the best data has been with psychosis. In the original project in western Finland over 75% of the people diagnosed with psychosis returned to study or work within two years of that episode – a figure greatly in excess of anything that is seen elsewhere.

There is a real move afoot to increase the extent of such practices in a number of acute treatment systems and I have come across several services that are beginning to look into the introduction of such cultures in their treatment settings. It is a bold step for clinicians – including myself – to take; they will have to be the first to work on dropping their ego mask for such an ethos to work, but the rewards for such work go far beyond anything that status could ever offer.

Every crisis is seen as enfolded within an opportunity, and the direction of travel is one that is agreed upon mutually, with as few prejudgements as possible. An open-minded attitude is needed for such innovative solutions to spread and take hold, and this may require, particularly for professionals, the willingness to question some fundamental assumptions at the heart of biological psychiatry.

To do this, we need to start by asking ourselves the most basic question of all: namely, what do we mean by mind? How tenable is it really to state – as the reductionist paradigm does – that the mental phenomena of mind that we experience are exactly the same as components of the brain itself? This is how science writer, Rita Carter puts it, in her book *Mapping the Mind*, 'The latest brain scans reveal our thoughts, memories, even our moods – as clearly as an X Ray reveals our bones.' Is that really true? A number of scientists and professionals take exception to this basic pillar of psychological medicine and neuroscience. The objections of Jeffrey Schwartz, an American professor of psychiatry, are laid out clearly in his book *The Mind and the Brain*,

> Even as Congress declared the 1990s the Decade of the Brain, a nagging doubt plagued some neuroscientists. Although learning which regions of the brain become metabolically active during various tasks is crucial to any understanding of brain function, this mental cartography seemed ultimately unsatisfying. Being able to trace brain activity on an imaging scan is all well and good. But what does it mean to see that the front of the brain is underactive in people with schizophrenia?
>
> . . . Neuroscientists have successfully identified the neural correlates of pain, of depression, of anxiety. None of those achievements, either, amounts to a full explanation of the mental

experience that neural activity underlies. The explanatory gap has never been bridged. And the inescapable reason is this: a neural state is not a mental state. The mind is not the brain, though it depends on the material brain for its existence (as far as we know). As the philosopher Colin McGinn says, 'The problem with materialism is that it tries to construct the mind out of properties that refuse to add up to mentality.'

What, to me, is being convincingly argued here is that, though we may be able to see parts of the brain activated at the same time as certain emotions are experienced, what does this really tell us? A crucial reality about our inner experiences, like thoughts and feelings, is that no one has ever seen them. This might sound obvious, but it's worth pausing to acknowledge this for a moment: thoughts and feelings are unseen. We may see some of their biological correlates, but this is not the same thing. For example, a part of the brain known as the amygdala appears to be activated when someone experiences anger. But when we look at the brain of an angry person – say, through a special MRI scan – and watch the amygdala light up, demonstrating an increased level of activity at that moment, do we really believe that we can 'see' the person's anger? Of course not. Anger comes in so many shapes and permutations and it is unique both to the person experiencing it, and the moment in which it is experienced. We are seeing something that correlates with it, but not the actual thing itself. Saying that the neural activity of an emotion is the same as the emotion itself is like saying that a signpost saying 'Welcome to Cambridge' is the same as the city of Cambridge itself.

This is the elephant in the room when it comes to neuroscience or, more specifically, the materialist neuroscientific interpretation of psychiatry. There is a giant leap being made between the biological and mental, the brain and the mind, and a huge piece of the puzzle is missing in our understanding. Even a number of neuroscientists appreciate this, and consequently are very open about the limitations of their own discipline. As the Canadian neuroscientist Dr Mario Beauregard wrote,

> The brain can be weighed, measured, scanned, dissected and studied. The mind . . . however, remains a mystery. It has no mass, no volume and no shape, and it cannot be measured in space and time. Yet it is as real as neurons, neurotransmitters, and synaptic junctions. It is also very powerful.

What we call mind here are the subjective elements of our experience, feelings and sensibilities that we have all the time but that can never fully be expressed with words. There seems to me to be a fundamental flaw in the reductionist notion that these experiences are somehow generated by the brain as if it were some kind of computer. Take, for example, the sensation of pain. You can describe what kind of pain it is (dull, sharp, throbbing and so on) and you can understand what brings it about, like touching a naked flame for example, which causes some tissue damage. And you can also understand how you normally react to it, which might, in this case, be to pull away and say 'ouch'. If you then feed all that information, in as much detail as possible, into a computer-controlled robot that is consequently programmed to react to pain in the same way you do – to pull away and say 'ouch' – in the same circumstances, can we honestly say that the robot is able to *feel* pain as a result? Again, of course not. The whole realm of subjective consciousness is the realm of the mind, and no amount of physical building blocks can ever fully create it, because it is not in itself part of our web of physical reality. Here's how the philosopher and writer Jim Holt puts it in his bestselling book *Why Does the World Exist?* 'Think of the way a pinch feels, a tangerine tastes, a cello sounds, or the rosy dawn sky looks. Such qualitative experiences – philosophers call them "qualia" – have an inner nature that goes beyond their role in the causal web.'

So that leaves us with the vexing question of what exactly this 'mind' is? We all walk around with, and forever experience the world through it, but where is it and how does it relate to our brains? In order to try and investigate this and develop an understanding of how it squares with my academic learning, as well as personal and clinical experiences, I had to re-examine the whole world view that my education had given me and, in so doing, I found myself going all the way back to the earliest days of my undergraduate studies.

One of the first aspects of neuroscience every medical student learns is something called the Penfield brain map. It is a functional representation of a couple of strips of the brain, just behind the frontal lobes, known as the motor cortex and the somatosensory cortex. The map itself involves drawings of different parts of the body adjacent to certain areas of the brain and they represent connections between those parts of the body and the brain. In the motor cortex, the parts of the brain concerned, when stimulated, activate movement in the corresponding parts of the body, and in the somatosensory cortex, each area of the brain is activated when the respective part of the body is touched. The map produced actually has a very odd look as various parts of the body are strikingly over-represented: the fingers, mouth and other sensitive areas take up most of the map because these are the areas that involve most intricate coordination when it comes to movement, or heightened sensation when it comes to sensory input.

This map was constructed in the 1930s by the neuro-surgeon Wilder Penfield and successive generations of medical students have had to commit the intricacies of this illustration to memory. Penfield drew up his map when he was operating on patients for severe epilepsy. During the procedure itself, he was able to allow patients to remain fully conscious and alert as brain tissue does not contain any pain or sense receptors. He conducted his brain-mapping experiments on thousands of patients by touching different parts of the brain with electrodes. In certain areas – which he subsequently mapped out – the touch would result in a rudimentary movement or twitch of the part of the body concerned, and in other areas a sensation would be elicited. This inspiring story of pioneering medical advancement has been routinely shared with almost every aspiring doctor over most of the last century. His findings are seen, in many ways, as one of the original exhibits of evidence in support of the reductionist material perspective of neuroscience. But there is an aspect of this story that I learnt only when researching this book – over a decade and a half after I left medical school – and it is one that, as far as I can make out, is almost universally omitted from the official telling.

Penfield observed that when patients chose to move a part of their body themselves, they would know and report that they deliberately did it. On the other hand, when that part of the body jerked into movement as a result of Penfield touching the relevant part of the brain, they would report, 'I didn't do it. You made me do it.' Thus, Penfield concluded, as reported in the book, *Brain Wars*, 'Higher mental functions – such as consciousness, reasoning, imagination and will – are not produced by the brain: mind is a nonphysical phenomenon interacting with the brain.'

Here, then, is a crucial pointer to what is perhaps the primary function of the brain. Our mental capacities are not necessarily something that equate with, or originate in, the brain itself, or indeed matter at all. If we think back to the observer effect of quantum physics, outlined in Chapter 5, it appears that the mental act of observation itself has an impact on the physical matter before it. In other words, it is the mental that is affecting the physical, rather than the other way round. A central shibboleth of the materialist paradigm is that consciousness and mind arise from matter, yet consistent findings such as these suggest the opposite. Far from being the creator of mind, then, it may well be the case that our brain is, in fact, the receiver of it. A metaphor that works for me is that of a television set. Our brains are the interface between the nonlocal and the local. There is a nonlocal aspect of mind, without boundaries, where separation does not exist, and it interfaces with the realm of physicality, time and space – it becomes local – through the brain. It is the brain that converts the intangible into the material; the unknowable into a digestible, knowable form; in other words, its job is what we always thought it was – to make sense of the world. It distils the nonlocal realm of mind, and its output is the personal, unique thinking mind that we all possess and all the judgements and realities that flow from it. And the only way that this thinking mind can operate is through the creation of ego, as described in Chapter 4. The perspective of the nonlocal function of our mind is boundless, whereas that of our thinking local mind is limited, like a form of tunnel vision. This nonlocal mind is thus more conscious than our individual thinking mind, which is, in many respects, a form of unconsciousness. And, of course, our thinking mind itself has many layers; parts of it are more unconscious than others. Indeed, it possesses some elements that we are blissfully unaware of most of the time but that, nevertheless, influence us heavily throughout our lives. But it is by travelling through all these layers that we are finally able to engage in 'clear seeing' as the Buddha put it. In other words, the route to our nonlocal mind is by looking into and through the machinations of the thinking mind, rather than looking out from it.

Our individual thinking mind is only able to see the world through the ego construct. It is only able to use the functions of our five senses and the notion of this 'I' we think we are, and so everything we think, feel, see, taste, touch or hear is a result and indeed a construct of our thinking mind. The thinking mind judges, analyses, ruminates, pontificates and cogitates, while the nonlocal aspect of mind observes. The local mind is about doing, while the nonlocal mind is just about being. There are ways to experience this universal, nonlocal aspect of mind, as I mentioned previously in Chapters 3 and 7, but the experience is not something we can clearly describe with words or prose of any kind. The best we can hope for, through the limited functions of our thinking mind, are pointers, using language and thought as the metaphors that they basically are. Thinking mind creates a box (ego) that our more conscious, nonlocal mind is contorted to fit within. It can be thought of as a filter that is narrowing down our field of consciousness and so, using the TV metaphor again, it's like a receiver that is able to pick up, mould and broadcast only a small range of channels out of the infinite possibilities that exist.

When we are intervening at the level of the physical brain, therefore, it is as if we are fiddling with the controls of the TV set. The medications we prescribe – to the extent that they exert their effects on the physical plane – can be seen as ways of tweaking the various parameters of the signal we receive, whether that be colour, volume, brightness, contrast or anything else. They, therefore, have an effect on the gross aspects of what we can see, and that is the reason for some of their efficacy. But it is, overall, a fairly blunt and limited efficacy. Indeed, the patients I have treated even describe the experience of psychiatric drugs in very similar terms; they will say they feel that their volume has been turned down, that their experience of life is less bright, vibrant or salient. A patient specifically said to me recently, 'This medication is not curing me, it's just blunting me.' It struck me that he knew exactly what he was talking about. Sometimes, however, this is necessary and preferable to the far greater distress they had been suffering prior to the medication, particularly where risk to the self or others is concerned. In terms of the wheel of awakening, they will be moving a couple of millimetres back in an anticlockwise direction from the position they had once become stuck in.

The problem, however, is that deep down, the original picture still remains the same. It has just been adjusted or camouflaged, if you like, to fit in with what they or society needed at the time. A vulnerability to slipping back into illness therefore remains, and this can happen at any time. This would explain the high relapse rate.

In my experience, while the physical effect of medication is able to act on the superficial and immediate level, psychological intervention (or, indeed, the placebo effect) works on deeper levels altogether; levels that go beyond that which is seen on the surface/ screen level of the television set. Every major branch of psychology has concerned itself with acting on levels of our thinking mind and, in particular, the vast array of phenomena that we are not normally even aware of. Indeed the genius of Freud's original insights was exactly this. Notions that psychiatrists take for granted, like the unconscious, and defence mechanisms, such as denial and projection, are also now common parlance in mainstream popular science and psychology. Freud shone a torch on a whole warehouse of our inner world that was driving much of our behaviour all along but which we had failed to notice or at least, up until that point, the scientific/professional community had failed to articulate. The ultimate format of the intervention he espoused – psychoanalysis – involved relatively free-floating sessions in which the client gradually developed awareness of his or her unconscious with essentially no more than very subtle nudges from the therapist. This makes for lengthy and intense work but, to my mind, there is little doubt that, where it can be afforded and engaged in, much benefit can be gained. There have been a number of fascinating and powerful off-shoots from the original standard Freudian intervention like that developed by his former student Carl Jung who, in turn, influenced other pioneering therapies like transpersonal and client-centred therapies. I have particular interest in and respect for these, particularly where an openness to the spiritual dimension of experience is concerned. Their provision has not been on the same scale as psychoanalysis but smaller training centres and practices have existed, and still do today, and I have engaged in a fair amount of my own education and personal development through them.

The psychological intervention that really took the baton from psychoanalysis, however, was cognitive behaviour therapy and this remains one of the most used forms of psychotherapy around the world today. CBT again is looking at the thoughts – often hidden – that underlie our behaviours and its aim is to help us unearth them and see where they might be faulty or unhelpful, and thus facilitate a change in behaviour and a reduction in distress.

All of these therapies are ways of increasing awareness of what is going on within the mind, beneath the surface, and so the basic objective is a deeper level of change than that achieved by medication alone. In fact there is now a lot of data, via randomized controlled trials, that demonstrates the value of many of these therapies – particularly CBT, where most of the recent research has been done – in reducing the relapse rate in conditions such as depression beyond that which would be achieved with medication alone.

Psychological therapy can, of course, be hard work and it thus requires cooperation from the client. Sometimes this is not forthcoming, in which case medication remains the only option, but engagement at this level should always be attempted wherever possible.

One of the more accessible modes of engagement at the mental level, however, is through one's system of religious beliefs. After all, if a significant proportion of the effects of medication can be attributed to a belief in the medication itself (as in the placebo effect), then surely a belief in a particular faith will have the same effect when it is used to assist treatment and improve wellbeing. This has actually been corroborated by a number of studies. In one such experiment, researchers from Massachusetts examined the extent to which psychiatric patients believed that their treatment would work and also believed in a God who would facilitate this healing process. After a one-year follow up they discovered that those who believed in a God aiding the treatment process had better outcomes than those who did not. They concluded, 'Our work suggests that people with a moderate to high level of belief in a higher power do significantly better in short-term psychiatric treatment than those without, regardless of their religious affiliation.'

Other studies have focused on the aspects of these beliefs that made a difference, and one such study reported in the *Journal of Clinical Psychology* that, 'Benevolent religious reappraisals were associated with perceptions of positive mental health, whereas punishing God reappraisals and reappraisals of God's power were associated with self-reported distress and personal loss.'

The effect that such spiritual beliefs have on mental illness and the course of treatment is well known to many, not least of all the patients themselves. In fact a survey of 339 patients in Los Angeles found that more than 81% of the participants reported using religious beliefs or activities to cope. A lack of interest in these aspects of a patient's life, especially if they volunteer it, is therefore a grave error on the part of any psychiatrist, as it may well come to represent a genuine missed opportunity. This is, of course, not in any way the same as a clinician forcing or even influencing the patient with their own views or beliefs; it is merely a case of being open to explore spiritual systems, and how they might help, but in a way that is initiated and fully guided by the patient.

For me, therefore, chaplaincy services are not merely an add-on or a tick-box exercise, when it comes to mental health; they are, in fact, an integral part of the treatment system itself. In Romania, for example, where Diana, my deputy, comes from, I understand that the psychiatric services work closely with local churches and they dovetail their efforts together nicely into a more seamless, combined provision that works synergistically.

I can't help wondering how much of this was once known but subsequently lost under the tsunami of anti-religious materialism and pharmaceutical company marketing that we have all been buried under in the West over the last half century. Outside this part of the world, however, spiritual practitioners are, by default, an integral part of the mental-health support system and outcomes seem to be all the more impressive because of it. This may be one of the reasons for the findings of the World Health Organization, which consistently, over several decades of study, has found that relapse rates in schizophrenia are lower in the developing world than in the West. Extended families and social networks are also likely to play a role in this too, and this is why the Open Dialogue focus on intervention at this level can be so powerful.

Spirituality is actually often a fundamental aspect of this and I have even heard stories from family members attesting to the power of the local religious elder in affecting a cure for a member of his congregation who suffered with what would normally be regarded as symptoms of a mental illness. One concerns a relative in a previous generation, who used to hear and see her husband on a regular basis shortly after he died in the First World War. Her husband began telling her not to go outside and feed the animals or tend the land she used to make a living from, assuring her that he was going to take care of it for her – as he would have done when alive. Consequently the family became very worried about her, as she slowly lost grip of her livelihood and ability to look after herself. She went to the local priest for some counsel, and after several months of this, and some discussion, he told her simply to turn her back to her husband next time he came, as it was now time for her to move on. And it was also time for him to go to God. She followed his simple instruction the following week and, according to the family, rapidly started to recover after that.

Indeed, from my extended family in Bangladesh, there are numerous stories of people beginning to recover from various forms of acute psychological disturbance after a religious ceremony involving family members and the local imam. Belief, therefore, is central to the healing process and, without it, even the physical treatments we prescribe are likely to have limited effect. Most psychiatrists, for example, find themselves hard-pushed to explain why some patients will respond to a particular drug while others don't and why some appear treatment-resistant altogether. On my ward we are never able to predict who will respond to which medication and when. We try and we hope and, as much as possible, we try to engage with the patient and their family as well – even through the acute psychosis – and that, to my mind, is what likely makes all the difference. Here, too, there are plenty of studies that show the effect of the therapeutic relationship on treatment efficacy itself. Stefan Priebe and Rosemary McCabe of Queen Mary College, University of London, found, in a review of numerous treatment-outcome papers that, 'The therapeutic relationship is a reliable predictor of patient outcome in mainstream psychiatric care.' The more an individual suffering mental illness is able to relate to those looking after her, the more able she might be to accept the advice that is being given to her and, hence, believe in the treatment itself. In many respects, in the West today, the clinicians and scientists have replaced the pastors and clergy that still exist elsewhere and, as a result, the treatment response is significantly related to the patient's relationship to, and respect for, the staff.

All of this points to the importance of working at a deeper mental level, rather than leaving it to chemicals alone. Of course, belief systems can become barriers to progress too and that is why their deployment needs to be done intelligently, on the basis of utility alone. Will this belief system serve healing or hinder it? I am always, therefore, open to challenging a patient's belief system too, if it is leading them to do harm to themselves or others, but I rarely have to stray too far from the patient's own perspective to do so, for in most mainstream religious beliefs, the importance of kindness and doing unto others as one would do to one's self is firmly embedded.

The world of psychology is increasingly opening up to a dialogue with, and acceptance of, religious beliefs where they serve the healing process, rather than coming from a perspective of its own materialist dogma as had previously been the case. Freud had a distinctly frosty relationship with religion and it tends to be reflected in psychoanalysis, although many modern practitioners have a much more open-minded approach. Indeed, the more modern therapies like CBT have no inbuilt aversion to religious belief systems at all; again, it's all about what works and what reduces distress.

But for all the advances made in the psychological realm, it does have to be said that it too still has its own limitations. We have to be honest about the fact – and most psychologists are – that there are many people for whom these interventions ultimately do not work. As Professor David Kingdon – academic and consultant psychiatrist from the University of Southampton – pointed out in the journal *The Psychiatrist* some years ago, many questions around these core interventions still remain:

> Even when a therapy course is completed, 'treatment resistance' is well recognized; CBT does not work with every patient. Why do some patients find it helpful whereas others do not? Why do some patients drop out prematurely? At what point in therapy should a decision be made that CBT, as offered, is not appropriate or sufficient?

Such concerns exist around all forms of psychological therapy and engagement on the mental level and, for me, the reason is that, basically, all these interventions are seeking to heal the thinking mind from within the thinking mind itself. Their main benefit is that, unlike medication, we are going deeper, behind the screen to alter the mechanics of the television set, as it were. The basis of the intervention, however, still sits within the ego paradigm through which our thinking mind experiences the world and, as a result, it can easily unravel itself. We may be able to use language and logic to challenge the harmful underlying thoughts we walk round with in life but there's nothing to stop another new set of thoughts, beliefs and concepts simply washing in and superseding them, sending us back into another spiral of despair. Ultimately, although using the thinking mind to cure the thinking mind may have a deeper and longer-lasting effect than merely using pharmaceutical agents that act at the biological interface alone, this may well still not provide the permanent solution from suffering that people seek.

What we need, then, is a method that does not rely on the thinking mind/ego paradigm at all. A method that operates quite literally 'outside the box'. This very notion, of course, generates a couple of profound questions. If the thinking mind is the fundamental basis of everything we see, hear, touch, taste, smell and think, then how can such a method ever be found? How can there be an intervention that is based on nothing that we can ever know?

In fact such a method has been used for over 2,500 years. It has been practised by millions of people throughout the intervening millennia, and the modern worlds of mental and physical health care have been increasingly waking up to its profound and widespread benefits. I will outline it in the next chapter.

Chapter 13
The Mindfulness Movement

'The cessation of suffering is attainable.'

The Buddha

THE FOUR NOBLE TRUTHS are the core message of the Buddha's teaching. He starts with a universal declaration that life means suffering. To live is to suffer. The second Noble Truth is that the origin of this suffering is attachment. This is a key insight into exactly how the mind works. It always wants something that it does not have in this very moment. This continual reaching outward is the fundamental nature of mind. If it was not for this yearning, there would be no suffering, as we would be content with what we have right here, right now. In the next two Noble Truths the Buddha moves to the optimistic dimensions of insight. He says that a cessation of this suffering is actually attainable, and in the fourth Noble Truth he lays out a path via which this cessation of suffering can be attained. This is known as the Eightfold Path and central to it is what he calls Right Mindfulness.

Mindfulness is about seeing things in clear consciousness. And contrary to what we might think, it actually requires a lot of practice. The grasping mind is constantly sabotaging our ability to see anything clearly. If you don't believe me then try and focus your attention on a single ordinary item before you – say, a glass or the leg of a chair or a pen – for five minutes. You'll find that your mind soon takes you away from pure focus. In fact, you don't even need to do it because you know it'll be almost impossible. There is nothing you're able to perceive without your mind getting in the way. Yet, we somehow fool ourselves into thinking that we are actually able to perceive the world as it is, as pure objective reality. The truth for all of us, however, is that everything we perceive is inevitably wrapped up in constructs of our own mind. Memories, assumptions, thoughts and feelings swirl around everything we experience; we are forever relating every item we encounter to others, via aspects of our inner mental world. Clear seeing is the realization, therefore, that no perception we have is wholly objective. It is all, to one degree or another, a construct of mind. Mindfulness is thus the ability to notice that everything we are observing is, in fact, being seen through the prism of mind. This means not just being aware of the object we are perceiving, but also being aware of the mind that is perceiving and interacting with it too.

Mindfulness is not an all or nothing quality, we all have it to degrees, and we are all capable of being more or less mindful at different times. Whenever we have an impression that what we believe is a totally objective view of reality, that's when we are being less mindful. What is happening here is that we are looking out from mind – as if it somehow didn't exist – without realizing that it is always present, and we are always seeing everything through it. This is the trap that fundamentalists of every creed fall into – whether religious or scientific. They believe that their perception is illuminated only by the totally clear light of reality, not realizing that what is actually illuminating every one of their perceptions is their mind. Without the mind there could be no perception and no opinion.

A high level of mindfulness is thus strongly correlated with a high level of emotional intelligence. Emotional intelligence is an awareness of one's own emotional terrain, which in turn helps one gain an awareness of the emotional terrain of others too. This is the inevitable outcome of a mindful approach. Emotions are never denied. They may not always be acted upon, for sure, but the truth that they are front and centre of our experience is never avoided. This means that when we're being mindful, we are always being respectful of the feelings and opinions of others around us because we know that our impressions are just that, impressions, and never unassailable realities. Mindfulness thus brings about empathy and compassion for others. Most importantly, of course, it also brings about a compassion for oneself, because that's where true compassion has to start.

Mindfulness practice tends to start with the observation of something – usually the breath – for sustained periods of time. Some people think that the idea is to free your mind of thoughts but nothing could be further from the truth. As soon as you start to pay attention to what is normally considered mundane, your mind will kick in and try and take you anywhere but in the present moment. Thoughts or fantasies about the future or memories or concerns about the past will rise up and, before you know it, the object you are paying attention to will be the furthest thing from your mind. But that's OK. That's meant to happen. That's exactly how our mind works. The key is to bring the attention back, again and again and again. This will make you aware of what the Buddha referred to as the first foundation of mindfulness, which I briefly outlined earlier, namely that, when we pay attention to something, we can either find the experience pleasant, unpleasant or neutral. The second foundation of mindfulness that flows from this is that if something is perceived as neutral (like, say, our breathing), ceasing to pay attention to it will, over time, lead us to find it unpleasant, and the corollary is also true in that, if we pay sustained attention to a perception that we consider to be neutral, it will, over time, become pleasurable.

In these first two principles we can learn so much about our own attitude to ourselves. Our self-esteem is directly related to the amount of attention we pay to ourselves. When we're constantly juggling with life and rushing from one task to the next, we leave very little time just to sit with and pay attention to our bodies and our inner world. This leads us to find our own company less and less pleasurable and so we need to make more and more effort to keep busy with other things and other people. In other words, the more we run away from ourselves, the more we will want to run away from ourselves. We can, however, choose to break this cycle any time. If it's even for two minutes a day, that's a start. Paying attention to yourself will gradually build up the positive feeling you have for yourself and, over time, you will enjoy that time more and more. It takes practice and effort, though, without doubt. After several years of meditating, I started to find that it was something I looked forward to. Although my mind still tries to distract me from it all the time, I can still usually sense a great joy at the prospect of sitting quietly and paying attention to myself. Now I understand what the Buddha meant when he said, 'You yourself as much as anyone in the Universe deserve your love and attention.' This is perhaps my favourite quote from him.

Another misconception about mindfulness meditation is the idea that it involves the immediate experience of pure peace, bliss or joy. Again, it is anything but this, at least for the most part, and certainly to start with. It is about opening ourselves up to whatever is going on inside, and that is not always pleasant. Sticking with it through all that arises is really the ultimate compassion. It is about being steadfast with ourselves. One of my favourite writers, Pema Chodron, talks about this quality of steadfastness in her wonderful book *The Places that Scare You*,

> When we practise meditation we are strengthening our ability to be steadfast with ourselves. No matter what comes up . . . we develop a loyalty to our experience. Although plenty of meditators consider it, we don't run screaming out of the room. Instead we acknowledge that impulse as thinking, without labelling it right or wrong.

So, in the most fundamental way, it's about facing up to ourselves rather than following our natural tendency to run away. The more we do it the less, over time, we fear our own reactions. And the less we fear our own reactions, the less we fear, well . . . anything. I remember once after a particularly challenging week-long silent meditation retreat, coming away with the feeling that I no longer had to be so afraid of fear. It was one of the most liberating moments of my life. As President Franklin Roosevelt said, 'The only thing we have to fear is fear itself.' If you no longer fear your own fear, then, at one level, you no longer fear anything. It is not that we can ever avoid experiencing fear or irritation or anger or pain, but it is about being able to hold all of these things, and still carry on with what is important to our lives. This is what Susan Jeffers talks about in one of the bestselling self-help books ever, *Feel the Fear and Do It Anyway*. In a quintessentially American way, she managed to communicate the whole idea beautifully in the space of her title!

This is also what the Buddha referred to as the middle way, between suppressing our desires, needs, drives, yearning and feelings on the one hand, and indulging them on the other. It is about being present – allowing them to be and just experiencing them for what they are, without words, judgements, analyses or conclusions. And, at base, this is a process of being with our bodies. Mindfulness is about delving deeper into our inner world, beneath the layer of words and cognitions. In this preverbal space, where there are no stories or narratives flying round to tell us what is what, or interpret or relate every last thing, there is only pure feeling, pure physical sensation that can be located within the body. This is what Eckhart Tolle refers to as 'the pain body'. The body is like a reservoir of pain, emotional accumulations that we have not attended to for decades, and it's all still in there.

When I was undergoing training to become a mindfulness teacher myself, in the Zen tradition, a fellow student of the training once told me how he had observed other students, who happened to be from the mental-health professions, always trying to help others by getting them to understand their thoughts and behaviours intellectually in the context of their lives – 'examining the entrails' as he put it – when, in fact, our training was teaching us the deeper value of going direct to the body itself, and cutting out the middle man of thought, as it were. Indeed some highly illuminating scientific evidence has emerged to back this up in recent years. In her wonderful book *Molecules of Emotion*, Professor Candace Pert reveals how her decades of academic research in psychoneuroimmunology have taught her how a panoply of chemicals in the body, known as neuropeptides, seem to be the messengers of emotion. Sometimes they pass their messages up to the brain via the nervous system, but, more usually, they just sit in the organs where they form or circulate in response to the stimuli and stressors that the organism experiences. In her book, she puts it thus:

> Peptides and other informational substances are
> the biochemicals of emotion, their distribution
> in the body's nerves has all kinds of significance,
> which Sigmund Freud, were he alive today, would

gleefully point out as the molecular confirmation of his theories. The body is the unconscious mind!

The process of meditation, therefore, is one of floating in the reservoir of emotion that is our body, knowing and experiencing it for what it is. This is the fuel that has driven so much of our perspective on life and the cycles we have travelled. And by immersing ourselves in it, we start to notice the world differently and we realize that this reservoir is, in some senses, actually all there is; nothing is separate from it. Such immersion into the body provides us with a different way of knowing and experiencing the world, one that is fundamentally different from the lens of intellect generated by the thinking mind.

The Zen tradition, like several others, in fact takes this further, continuing the process beyond the meditation cushion. This teaches methods of sustaining mindfulness of the body in all waking hours. My teacher, Daizan Roshi, uses the analogy of pulling a silk thread. To get the most out of it, one needs to use a smooth, constant flowing motion, and so it is with mindfulness. With a persistent approach it can become truly transformative.

And as a result, we become ever more aware of this well of emotion we carry with us at all times. But instead of being something to avoid, it turns out that within it is the very path to our liberation. This underlying well of emotion is what the Buddha referred to as our 'mind state'. And, like any dynamic fluid, it is in a perpetual state of flux, ebbing and flowing always. As a result, we will experience it in various ways at different times. Sometimes it will feel bright and positive and at other times it will feel dark and negative. The underlying vibration of the mind state acts as a kind of coloured lens through which all our experiences are filtered. This is the Buddha's third foundation of mindfulness. Everything we experience is filtered through the lens of our mind state. And perhaps the most profound paradox of all is that only when we accept that we are entirely unable to perceive anything in purely objective terms will we start being able to see more clearly. We cannot know reality in all its fullness – certainly not with the mind and five senses we have at our disposal – but the knowledge that we can't know this way becomes itself a giant window onto the deeper levels of reality.

Over time, we learn to see without seeing and know without thinking – using the body too, rather than the brain alone – and the more we do, the more we come to realize that wherever we go, every experience we are having is fundamentally an experience of our own selves. As Jon Kabat-Zinn put it, in the title of one of his bestselling books, 'Wherever you go, there you are.' Seeing clearly is hence, in every sense, a method of self-discovery. And the more we do this, the more we expand our consciousness – slowly dismantling the box of ego, bit by bit.

This brings us back to the television metaphor. Both psychological and pharmacological interventions clearly have their place, depending particularly on the severity of the problem at hand. They each operate at different levels – on the surface/screen, or within the box itself – and in the most severe situations change is only possible through medication. Such interventions must also, wherever possible, be provided within a collaborative framework where family members and social networks work in partnership with clinicians who approach every case with an open mind. Then, after the acute phase is over, in order to achieve a truly lasting and irreversible effect, and one that authentically keeps the individual moving in an anticlockwise direction on the wheel, towards ever deepening awakening, a regular mindfulness practice should ideally be introduced also. Mindfulness is a way of gently dismantling the ego construct, which is where the problem manifested in the first place, step by step – thereby increasing resilience in the deepest sense. It is as if we are slowly opening the TV set up so it is able to receive more and more channels from the infinite streams available, rather than remaining stuck on the narrow band of stations it had been restricted to up till now. Consciousness expands as we become more and more open to experiencing reality beyond the narrow ego-based paradigm to which we had hitherto been fused. It is little wonder, therefore, that mindfulness has been continually practised for the last couple of thousand years by various communities of people around the planet; it is basically a treatment for the human condition itself.

Indeed, there are a number of studies now that show the direct effect that mindfulness has on the structure of the brain. Harvard University academic psychologist Sara Lazar, for example, performed MRI scans on the brains of 20 meditators with an average of nearly 3,000 hours of mindfulness practice and compared them to 15 non-meditators. She found an increase in grey-matter thickness in the brains of the meditators that was proportional to the amount of time spent meditating:

> Our data suggests that meditation practice can promote plasticity in adults in areas important for cognitive and emotional processing and well-being . . . In other words, the structure of an adult brain can change in response to repeated practice.

Another Harvard research psychologist, Britta Holzel, went about it a different way in that she recruited 16 meditation-naïve participants into a study which involved carrying out structural MRI scans before and after they embarked upon an eight-week course of Mindfulness-Based Stress Reduction (MBSR) and she compared this with a control group of 17 individuals who did not practise meditation at the outset and did not go through the course either. She found that only the MBSR group showed increased grey matter density in regions implicated in learning, memory, empathy and emotion regulation. The controls showed no change.

So mindfulness works across the board, on the spiritual, mental and physical levels, and this is why, over the last couple of decades, it has become increasingly incorporated into the world of psychological therapy. The number of controlled trials into the efficacy of mindfulness, across a variety of disorders, has recently mushroomed to produce an evidence base that is fast outstripping even the wildest expectations of its earliest proponents.

The key challenge for mindfulness practice, though, is starting it. It can be even harder to engage in than psychology, even though it is a personal practice that involves no therapists, no drugs and, therefore, no cost. Everyone recognizes how hard it is when they try it for the first time and, indeed, it took me years before I was able to practise it on a regular basis. This is why many of the new therapies have devised innovative formats to help people derive some of the benefits of a mindful approach, even before they may be ready to start their own practice. Collectively these have come to be known as 'third-wave' cognitive therapies, and one of the first of these formal schools to emerge was known as Dialectic Behaviour Therapy (DBT). Unlike normal behaviour therapy, DBT starts from a point of radical acceptance and validation of a client's current situation and capabilities, while at the same time acknowledging the need for change. It is through the tension of being with what is, that client and therapist then work cooperatively to evolve together one step at a time towards gradual change, but all within the context of a deeply accepting environment. DBT has shown remarkable success, particularly in patients with high rates of self-harm and suicidal thoughts, and borderline personality disorder.

Professor Jon Kabat Zinn from the University of Massachusetts Medical School is one of the pioneers of mindfulness-based interventions in mental health. He originated two forms of therapy known as Mindfulness-Based Stress Reduction and Mindfulness-Based Cognitive Therapy. They each involve group work over about eight weeks, in which a series of mindfulness skills are gradually taught to the attendees, deepening their ability for mindful engagement over time. Although these interventions are relatively new some solid evidence is already emerging around the benefits of MBCT, for example, in recurrent depression. One major controlled trial, for instance, showed that, when added to existing treatment, it significantly reduces the relapse rate for depression in those who have experienced three or more episodes of depression in the past.

Other third-wave treatments include Compassion Focused Therapy and its close cousins Functional Analytic Therapy and – my own particular favourite – Acceptance & Commitment Therapy (ACT). Professor Steven Hayes of the University of Nevada, whom I am pleased to call a friend, is its originator and a professional community, known as the Association of Contextual Behavioural Science (ACBS), has built up around ACT that is one of the fastest-growing professional bodies in the world of mental health today. I usually go to their annual conferences and it feels like their attendance almost doubles every year.

The genius of ACT is that it uses a series of metaphors to help people develop mindfulness skills. A key one is that of quicksand. A natural human tendency, when mired in quicksand, is to struggle to try and climb out of it. But, of course, the more we move our legs, the more we end up digging ourselves ever deeper into it. The way, in fact, to get out of quicksand is to do the counter-intuitive thing and lie across it; that way you can slowly start to roll out of it. This is a very powerful analogy for our inner world of thoughts and emotions.

They may not be to our liking but trying to avoid them is the one sure-fire way to becoming mired every more deeply into them. The best way to deal with them is to open ourselves up to them and just allow them to be. That which we accept we are no longer in conflict with, and when we are no longer in conflict with something, we are no longer controlled by it.

This is one of the many innovative images ACT uses in the therapeutic process, and exercises built around them are usually combined with a commitment to the client's values and goals that, regardless of what ever whirlwinds may be swirling inside, can always be maintained. It's a bit like driving a car. You can have some mirrors in front of you, reminding you of the past and all the ups and downs behind you, while at the same time keeping your eye on the road and moving ever forward in the direction of your choice.

I have conducted research on the use of ACT-based interventions in acute mental health myself and one of the trials I ran, based on a service I still provide in my ward, was around a daily ACT-based mindfulness group for both staff and patients alike. Some of the feedback I have received from these groups is unlike anything I have ever experienced in my career in psychiatry. One patient, for example, told me that 'I know that I would never have ended up here in hospital, or even prison before it, if I had learnt these skills before.' I have seen patients who almost evangelize to other patients about its benefits and I have read similar reports in a number of published papers around numerous mindfulness-based techniques. One published in the *Behavioural and*

Cognitive Psychotherapy Journal, entitled 'Participants' Experiences of Mindfulness-Based Cognitive Therapy', quoted a patient as saying, 'It changed me in just about every way possible.'

All this spurs me on to continue my quest to find ever more accessible avenues to help people engage in mindfulness practice. One such innovation that I designed to go with this book is a free online self-help resource that is for anyone who wishes to dip their toe slowly and steadily into the mindfulness water. It is a simple bite-sized guided mindfulness practice designed as a gentle way to help introduce you to regular practice and it can be found at www.1mindfulmoment.com. It is called Mindful Moment Training and involves a brief online presentation, incorporating a guided meditation that is less than five minutes long. Practising this exercise on a daily basis – which is not dissimilar to the way I started my own mindfulness practice – can, I believe, be a good starting point that you can gradually build upon over time. I will talk more at the end of the book about the online and offline resources that I have set up for those who might be interested.

The core message for me is that practice is key. At the end of the day one could read a hundred books on mindfulness but it is only through a sustained effort to engage in a regular practice that one starts to understand what it is all about. And the understanding that is gleaned is not an intellectual knowing; it is a knowing that operates at a far deeper level than our ordinary thinking mind, and the more we practice, the deeper that connection becomes. And, ultimately, the more deeply we connect with the level of our being beyond ego, the more we are able to choose. Because, essentially, mindfulness is about reclaiming our free will. We will never be rid of our ego, but, because we will be better at seeing it, we will start to enter into a skilful relationship with it. Some of what is going on in our thinking mind we might wish to go with, whereas other thoughts, instincts and impulses we may choose not to act upon. The more mindful we are, the less instinct-driven we become and the freer we are to choose our own destiny. In many senses, this is as much about enhancing 'free won't' as it is about free will. Interestingly, Professor Jeffrey Schwartz talks about exactly this when relating the successful mindfulness-based Four-Step therapy he designed for the treatment of OCD. 'In a nutshell, free won't refers to the mind's veto power over brain generated urges – exactly what happens when OCD patients follow the Four Steps.'

The core quality that this engenders is one of equanimity. Equanimity must never be mistaken for apathy. Someone who has equanimity cares deeply but does not allow the emotion to overwhelm her. As a *dharma* teacher once taught me, 'Equanimity is about being affected but not disturbed.' While the ripples at the surface of life continue to flutter, you are like the depth of the lake, wholly aware of the ripples, but, all the while, still at your core. Indeed, the more we identify with these deeper levels of life, the more connected we will feel with the whole of it. If we live our lives like the ripples on the surface, we will feel increasingly separate from the rest of the lake, as if we were isolated forms, but the more we spend time with our inner world, the more we will be able to identify with the most profound levels of reality, where the illusion of separation becomes increasingly evident. Compassion is thus a fundamental consequence of this realization yet, at the same time, on a practical level, it is also a pathway to realization in itself.

Chapter 14
Cultivating Compassion

'If you want others to be happy, practise compassion. If *you* want to be happy, practise compassion.'

The Dalai Lama

ONE OF THE MAJOR CONSEQUENCES of a regular mindfulness practice is the development of self-compassion. On the one hand we realize just how unruly we are deep down inside and that's what makes the practice difficult, but, on the other hand, the fact that we stick with it and spend this time with ourselves each day means that we can forgive ourselves this unruliness. Mindfulness is thus a way of practising regular kindness towards ourselves. This is beautifully articulated by Pema Chodron in her book *The Wisdom of No Escape*. Practices such as this help us realize that,

> We can still be crazy after all these years. We can still be timid or jealous or full of feelings of unworthiness . . . it's about befriending who we are already . . . Our brilliance, our juiciness, our spiciness, is all mixed up with our craziness and our confusion.

It is clear why the cultivation of this attitude can be immeasurably healthy for someone who has experienced mental illness but in exactly the same way it is good for all of us too. By increasing the levels of compassion we possess for ourselves, our compassion for others grows over time as well. When we realize there is so much darkness inside us we cannot but show understanding when we see this same energy resonating, in various forms, within others too. The very practice of compassion is itself perhaps one of the most powerful spiritual practices there is.

Christina Feldman, a well-known teacher in Western Buddhist circles, observed in a workshop of hers I once attended how compassion was an activity that involved the least 'selfing' of all. In most activities there is a very strong sense of the 'I'. We often spend time pontificating on things we have done in the near or distant past, 'How could I have done this?' or 'Why did I do that?' or 'What made me act that way?' but this doesn't happen so much after an act of kindness. We don't tend to go back over it and wonder what possessed us to be kind. In fact we don't spend much time thinking about 'me' at all, either during the act or after it.

So the very act of engaging in kindness to others is itself a method for gradually dissolving the ego. Indeed, probably knowing how hard a regular mindfulness practice could be for most people, the Buddha spent most of his time simply teaching kindness. As the Dalai Lama has said, 'My religion is very simple, my religion is kindness.'

Kindness means recognizing a kinship with another being, indeed that is where the meaning of the word came from in the first place; it is the appreciation that you are both 'of a kind'. In other words, it is an implicit acknowledgement of the lack of any real separation between us.

Before we go any further, however, we need to be clear about the difference between compassion and pity. When you pity someone you feel yourself to be above them. Pity does not have the quality of a joint experience; it is more about feeling sorry for someone, rather than sharing an experience with them. Pity can exist without much empathy but compassion cannot. Again, Pema Chodron illustrates this well too,

> Compassion is not a relationship between the healer and the wounded. It's a relationship between equals. Only when we know our own darkness well can we be present with the darkness of others. Compassion becomes real when we recognize our shared humanity.

And this is why compassion is such an essential quality, not just for patients, but for clinicians too. This might sound surprising, but if you look at the training and professional development structures that exist for most health-care professionals, you will find little or no emphasis on the maintenance and cultivation of one's own level of compassion. It is almost as if society is assuming that on becoming a doctor, a nurse or a psychologist you will walk out of college an immediately compassionate person and, no matter how many years you have been in your job, that will never waver for a day. The truth, as we all know, is that although all of us have a deep-seated inner compassionate dimension, we need to make an active effort to keep cultivating it. Faced with often very powerful explosions of ego, it can be hard to prevent our own egos joining in and reacting with their own venom, and before we know it a mutually destructive dance will have ensued. I have seen such cycles lead patients to get sucked ever deeper into the psychiatric system and much of it could have been prevented if the clinicians involved were able to keep their own egos in check at various stages, and not react in ways that then unconsciously exacerbated the situation again and again.

Freud was acutely aware of such dangers when he talked about the need for clinicians to be aware of their own 'counter transference', which meant the reactions that they felt were evoked by the patient within themselves. An awareness of this will reduce the chance of one then acting from these underground emotional streams when organizing a patient's treatment. Otherwise we risk contravening the first principle of the Hippocratic Oath, which all psychiatrists had to sign up to on qualifying as doctors, namely, 'Do no harm.'

The eminent British psychiatrist Dr Mike Shooter articulates this danger well:

> We are asked to treat with unconditional regard those patients who may irritate, frighten or appal us by their behaviour . . . It may cause us to confront all those unresolved issues in our own lives whose pain we have suppressed in the guise of helping others.'

As a result, many of us end up engaging in what a colleague has called the 'endless retreat from patients'.

On this basis, a mindfulness practice for clinicians is a win–win, and in the talks and workshops I give to psychiatrists on mindfulness, I emphasize how a regular practice will be as valuable to the doctor as it is to his or her patient. Indeed beyond doing no harm, I believe that cultivating compassion in a clinician can also have a profound and direct therapeutic effect itself. To be really compassionate you have to be willing to open yourself up to your own pain and, once you do this, you will be better at opening up to the patient's too. This is why, once this skill is developed, it can make a truly significant difference to the outcomes of patients. I find myself often inwardly resisting opening myself up to my patients' suffering, but when I bring awareness to this and start to share the emotional turmoil the person before me is experiencing, it often has a noticeable effect.

An excellent *dharma* teacher I once learnt from, Alan Lewis, talks about how, in the days when he was a senior Buddhist monk in Sri Lanka, providing pastoral support to his local community from the temple where he lived, people would often come to him with the most heart-wrenching problems. What he found was that, instead of engaging his thinking mind in a rush to remove their problems, when he opened his heart up to share what they were going through emotionally 'a kind of intelligence would emerge from the moment'. It is almost as if the sharing of pain births a new energy between you.

I remember sitting with a patient once who was telling me in a very distressed way about the voices he was hearing. He was in a highly agitated state and I knew, because of the timing of these voices, that they had something to do with some recent family stress he had been undergoing. He had not long become estranged from his wife and children and there appeared to be very little prospect of their reunion. I felt myself resisting the extreme anxiety he was emitting in that moment, as he talked of the disturbing nature of the voices coming to him, but then I made an extra effort to open up inwardly and allow myself to share his feeling. The very moment I did this, he began crying and much of the stress and emotional turmoil that was contributing to his symptoms started to pour out. He began telling me how he was missing his wife and children and how, even though he knew they couldn't reconcile, that was all he wanted to do. The tension that had been fuelling the voices streamed through him and the more he talked the lighter he felt. Nursing staff reported to me that he had appeared a lot brighter and less evidently disturbed for the rest of that day and, indeed, this coincided with somewhat of a turning point in his recovery.

Keeping myself open this way is, however, a continuing inner struggle. An effort always needs to be made to stay as present and attentive as possible and it will undoubtedly remain a career-long struggle. But it is a good struggle, and that itself is the beauty of my job. Every day with every new patient it forces me to grow, and by being more attentive to myself, I can be more attentive to my patients.

And I know, of course, that I am not the only one who is benefiting from this line of work in this way. This kind of cultivation of compassion creates virtuous cycles in which better clinicians keep producing better results for their patients. I did a study to examine this a couple of years ago. We sent round about 60 questionnaires to a variety of clinical staff – psychiatrists, nurses and other therapists – and we examined their level of mindfulness and self-compassion. We used a well-known rating scale that detects core mindfulness skills – known as the Freiburg Inventory. We then compared this to their therapeutic relationships with patients. What we found was that the higher the clinician's inner self-compassion and mindfulness skill (whether or not they knew what these things were called), the better their relationships were with their patients. So the more of these qualities a clinician possessed, the more harmonious and constructive their relationships were with the people they treat. And there is, of course, a lot of evidence to support a link between this and the speed and depth of the individual's recovery too. Indeed, a further study looked at treatment outcomes for clients of psychotherapists in training who practice mindfulness meditation, and compared them to the outcomes for clients of trainee therapists who don't. Fascinatingly they found 'significantly higher' outcomes in the clients of those who meditate.

Results such as these have spurred me to promote mindfulness practice across the field of health care, and I have now established a not-for-profit organization known as *The College of Mindful Clinicians* (www.

mindfulcollege.com). Its purpose is to help clinical staff to cultivate their compassion through commitment to a regular mindfulness practice. The first advertisement for it that I put in the *British Journal of Psychiatrists* received an overwhelming response. I had more than twice as many applicants as I had places for on the retreat. That first retreat was a resounding success and the College of Mindful Clinicians is now rapidly growing into a major association and resource for clinicians – across all disciplines and all areas of health care – and it is ultimately deeply beneficial, not only to the clinicians themselves, but also to the men, women and children whom they care for. My expectation is that this will eventually have a system-wide effect too, where cultural shifts, such as that represented by the Open Dialogue approach, will come a lot easier in areas where clinicians have established their own mindfulness practice.

Developing such inner compassion enables one to operate more from a place of humility and less from ego. This means that we will deploy value judgements less and in mental health, as we have discussed, this can be profoundly beneficial. The risk of seeing some-one merely as a diagnosis or a set of symptoms is always profound and when this happens the patient will instantly feel it. As a result, an immediate negative chemistry is injected into the relationship and this is ultimately detrimental to both client and clinician. Connecting with someone's suffering at a preverbal level thus has deep-seated benefits and often it leads the sufferer to feel known, understood and held for perhaps the first time.

The people who come to me in acute services for treatment from prison, for example, will often approach the relationship in a combative mood, ready to push back against any psychiatric or illness definition. When they realize, however, that I am not operating on that level either, they often begin to rethink. I tell them that I am not there to tell them what is real or not real, what is normal or what is abnormal/illness, I only want to know how we can work together to reduce the level of violence or aggression they have been engaged in, either towards themselves or others. It takes time but, gradually, we work towards forging a partnership, one in which I often learn as much from them as they do from me.

After a lifetime of training in medicine and psychiatry, it actually requires quite an effort to engage with someone purely on a human level that doesn't involve templates, judgements or labels of any kind. The lower the level of assumptions one makes, however, the deeper the connection that can be forged. You can watch thoughts and notions arise within like 'He has this illness so he is likely to be thinking this,' or 'That statement sounds like this symptom,' but at the same time just let them float by, while the focus on the patient's real and unique experience is maintained. Even assumptions like 'He is not in reality, whereas I am,' can be a cause of disconnection. As we discussed in Part 2 of this book, reality is not as black and white as we think. We are all trapped in some kind of misjudgement as to what the nature of reality is – due to seeing it through the tunnel of ego – and so no one really has the right to say to someone else, 'You are mad and I am sane.' The focus should always be on utility: 'How can I help you?'

Operating in an open-hearted and compassionate way also helps you see through the resistance and ego eruptions that might occur, or even dominate the picture, and still find a way to connect to the wisdom that is still clearly glowing within. This way, rather than just writing people off as 'mad', or 'bad', we can still find ways to cooperate with them as we navigate the myriad pathways of treatment available. We can be more open about the pros and cons of medication – balancing that against the paramount imperative to reduce risk of harm to anyone – while at the same time, exploring possibilities for psychological engagement and, ultimately, a mindful approach to longer-term recovery and a gradual paring down of ego.

Such relationships represent a genuine opportunity for mutual growth and this is something that, interestingly, I was able to learn about during my junior doctor days, from senior colleagues who themselves had histories of mental illness. I once had a boss who really did thrive on forging relationships with her patients. I noticed that she was able to make deep connections with them and understand their suffering and, over time, I learnt that this was because she had suffered mental illness herself too. Each opportunity to heal another was, at the same time, an opportunity to heal herself.

Another good example of this is again that of Dr Mike Shooter, who is, in fact, a former President of the Royal College of Psychiatrists. He talks candidly about the lack of compassion he often experienced himself while undergoing treatment for his own bout of mental illness, and the value he placed on kindness wherever he found it. He has spoken of 'a therapist who valued me for what I was, rather than what so many people wanted me to be, at a time when I loathed myself and imagined that everyone must do likewise. It made me aware that it was this sensitivity that had carried me into psychiatry in due course.'

It is no wonder, therefore, that increasingly these days, people who have had experiences with mental illness are themselves becoming involved in the care and support of others. This is indeed a welcome development in the field in recent years. There are service-user networks such as the Anxiety Alliance, the Hearing Voices Network and many others in which people recovered or recovering from mental illness join with those suffering more acutely to create an environment of mutual support, sensitivity and encouragement.

All of this chimes exactly with the Buddha's finding over 2,500 years ago, that demonstrating compassion was as powerful and healing an activity as receiving it. The more we connect and share with others, the more we recognize our commonality – both the positives and the negatives – and the more we do this, the more we see ourselves in them and, indeed, in all there is. That's when we realize that being compassionate was the very purpose of our existence in the first place: Put simply, it's how you find yourself again.

Chapter 15

Transformation

'Sorrow prepares you for joy. It violently sweeps everything out of your house, so that new joy can find space to enter. It shakes the yellow leaves from the bough of your heart, so that fresh, green leaves can grow in their place. It pulls up the rotten roots, so that new roots hidden beneath have room to grow. Whatever sorrow shakes from your heart, far better things will take their place.'

Rumi

THERE IS NO REASON WHY recovery from a period of psychological distress should mean going back to where you were beforehand. We all learn and evolve through every experience we have in life and mental illness should be no different. In fact, I believe that such experiences can be so profound that they have the potential to serve as an energetic force that, once appropriately channelled, can propel you in the direction of awakening. This, for me, is perhaps one of the most important aspects of the wheel of awakening that I have been describing throughout this book. Although the forces that drive you in an anticlockwise direction, towards awakening through awareness, involve insight and deep self-work – and those that take you in the opposite, clockwise, direction involve trauma, drugs and abuse – mental illness, in my view, also has the power to kick-start you on the road to awakening itself. Harnessed properly, such experiences can facilitate a particularly powerful engagement in self-work that then helps significantly accelerate the journey towards awakening. And the same applies to all of us, whether we have experienced mental illness or not. Every moment of disappointment, distress or despair contains within it a kernel of energy, which, if channelled properly can serve as a fuel for the onward journey of awakening. Something of a pendulum effect occurs, in that the higher up in the clockwise direction you travel, the more momentum you will gain when travelling back in the other direction towards awakening.

Over time, through a series of ever more frequent awakening experiences, we can gently feel the ego, and the whole world paradigm that it brings about, shrink in size as we realize more and more that we are not just what we can see, touch, hear, smell, taste or think about. The unseen part of us is so much deeper than that which we process through our thinking mind. We will never, of course, be rid of our ego, as long as we have a physical body but, over time, the ego lens we carry is seen to be a less and less substantial part of us. We feel more holistically in tune with deeper layers of ourselves and so the ego part becomes less and less central. This brings about a happier, less harmful and more content existence on every level and such a transformation is as important for us on an individual level as it is on a societal and, indeed, species level.

Our ego is both a blessing and a curse. It enables us to appreciate the world and, indeed, ourselves in ways that would not otherwise be possible. The human ego is far larger than that of any other species. Animals may have a sense of 'I' but it is far smaller than ours. Experiences that we have on a daily basis are far less acute or even non-existent in other species. You just have to notice how an animal reacts when it looks at itself in the mirror: in most cases it is not aware that it is looking at something it would call 'me'. As a result, everyday concerns that we walk round with are entirely absent in the animal experience. Preoccupations like 'I don't like the way I look', for example, do not even register for any species other than ours.

This strong ego lens has given us the ability to harness nature and develop technology in a way that is unprecedented. But this has come with a price, namely an over-attachment to ego that is associated with a *sense* of detachment (though not an actual detachment) from the part of us that lies deeper than it. Through my journey of treating those who suffer from mental illness I have come to realize that, in a way, we are all suffering from a form of mental illness. My name for it is Egophillia – love of ego. It leads us to follow the illusion of ego to its ultimate extent, placing personal and material gain above all else, and chasing status or success as if that was all that mattered, all the while believing that somehow the perfect life we have been waiting for lies just round the corner. The result of this, paradoxically, is a less and less contented life. Like a drug user, addicted to heroin, we have become addicted to our egos, forever craving the next superficial hit, while remaining entirely oblivious to the path of destruction this leaves in its wake.

As a result, we are trapped in a cycle of consumption and consumerism that threatens our very survival as a species on this planet and yet, even as the climate starts to change noticeably from year to year and the predicted rise of sea levels becomes visible within our own lifetimes, we continue with our ego-driven habits unabashed.

The good news is that life will always survive. But the bad news is that we humans may not survive with it. It's up to us as to whether or not the form of existence called humankind continues, and the key is to relearn that which we have always known deep down inside. Namely, that this ego that we think we are is just a layer of reality and not the whole of it. It's more like the surface of a bubble, and no more permanent or substantial than that. It is important, valid, beautiful and worth having, but it is not where we begin and end. It is, therefore, for the sake of our species that we must work towards ever-deeper engagement with the boundless levels of ourselves. On one level we exist in the way we think we do, but on another level we don't at all. On this level every separate notion or entity is entirely illusory. To survive we must live in both worlds. Those who experience psychosis become disconnected from this world, whereas the rest of us become disconnected from our deeper selves. Both are, in some respect, forms of delusion.

Each and every one of us, therefore, has a role to play in the reintegration of being. Your own journey will mirror that of the world. This might not make sense to ego, but it doesn't mean that it is not true. Our ego should serve us, rather than the other way round. And as we awaken, we will realize that we can do just that: shape, wear and change our ego mask as if it were an item of clothing, to suit the needs of the time. We all do it all the time anyway, only it is driven by ego's needs rather than our own deeper reality. When we are with friends, our ego takes a certain shape and orientation, and this is different to how it is with family or colleagues. As we awaken we become more aware and thus more in control of this process, becoming more flexible and thus more open. This way we can avoid getting stuck on ideas, belief systems, preferences and prejudices and focus our energies on what's important to us, and how we can use our existence to serve others and, indeed, all of creation. Like our ego, our self-image, our beliefs, our ideas and characteristics should serve our purpose and not the other way round.

To achieve this we need to be vigilant of the ever-creeping influence of thinking mind. I am always aware that my thoughts – however impressive they may sometimes feel – are at risk of taking me down a blind alley. They are as likely to help me as they are to hinder me. That is why I am constantly working on my relationship with my thinking mind, trying to be ever more skilful in the way I use it. A *dharma* teacher of mine once used the analogy of a relative's blind and slightly demented dog which is always running up to them and barking at their feet. They have a loving relationship with it but also need to keep it in its place much of the time. This is the relationship, she suggested, we ought to have with our thinking mind.

Our thinking mind and the way it processes all our perceptions must be seen, heard and experienced, but it must always be taken with a pinch of salt. And this also applies, as I stated in the beginning, to everything you read in this book. The insights I have delivered here should assist many – in all parts of the cycle – on their journey towards awakening, but it must also be recognized as only a limited, partial view of the reality that underlies it. For, just like any word-based support, it is still a case of us trying to challenge the hegemony of mind from within the mind itself. As a result, though texts like this may be of great value, they will never be enough on their own. What is essential is practice.

As I have said before, no verbal description of mindfulness practice can ever do it justice. We all know that practical pursuits like riding a bike or playing football cannot be learnt from a book and the same applies, only fifty-fold, to mindfulness practice, for it is the most practical pursuit of all. It is the one thing that every human being can do at any time, and that is why it is also the most voluntary thing we can do. The desire to commit to regular practice comes from within. And, if and when you feel that desire, then there will be many avenues available to you for guidance. Mindful Moment Training is one of many available. In developing it, my objective was to make it absolutely as accessible as possible on all levels. This is why it is available free online. It begins with a very short guided meditation that includes some direct instruction, and then deepens over a couple of stages to help ease the listener into a practice. I have also provided some tips about how to graduate from there to build up a longer practice slowly.

So if you don't have your own practice and feel ready to start one, then you're most welcome to go to www.1mindfulmoment.com and return as often as you like. For those who are interested in a deeper exploration of the spiritual realm through mindfulness and related practices, I also plan to run Awakening Workshops. This will involve some direct mindfulness teaching among other exercises to help facilitate the attainment of ever-deeper states of awakening. Details on how to organize or book one of these can be found on my website (www.russellrazzaque.com). There is also a link from there to the website of a not-for-profit organization I have recently established called the Delphi Foundation (www.delphifoundation.com). The purpose of the Foundation is to develop innovative treatments for severe mental illness, and currently we are working on a package of fairly intensive psychological treatment, with a mindfulness element. My aim is to demonstrate that an intervention of this nature has the potential to be more effective than current modes of treatment in the long term at reducing rates of future relapse into severe illness, whether bipolar or psychosis. The Foundation runs on charitable donations with the ultimate objective of creating a strong enough evidence base for such treatments that they are eventually adopted as standard interventions across health services globally. And incidentally we are always on the look-out for help with the Foundation, whether it be in organization, research support or fundraising.

The underlying purpose of all of these projects is to facilitate the journeys of people on all parts of the circle, helping us all to wake up to the realization that, in fact, there is fundamentally no circle at all. In truth, there is only the single point in the centre that we all are, even if our minds make us think otherwise most of the time.

One of the key ways to collapse this illusion is trust. My first *dharma* teacher, Leela Sarti, taught that, however anxious we may be about the future, if we truly pay attention to this moment, then the next one will take care of itself. It is by being fully immersed in the present, and all it has to offer, that we gradually come back into touch with who we really are. And as we develop trust in ourselves, we learn to trust the universe too, growing in the realization that the two are, in fact, one and the same. And, thus, we slowly replace the paranoia that characterizes thinking mind – and which pervades so much of our worldviews and relationships – with what has been described as a *pronoia*, namely, the knowledge that the universe is, in fact, conspiring on our behalf. If I believe in anything, it is that. And to me, this realization is what awakening is all about.

So whatever turmoil or turbulence life presents to you, know that it has happened for a reason: you broke down so that you may wake up. You got lost so that you may find yourself again.

Acknowledgements

ALL BOOKS ARE AN EVOLUTION. The ideas behind this book evolved over a period of about a year as I played around with them in my head week after week. Fundamental to this process was a range of valued colleagues whom I bounced the ideas off from time to time. The more I talked things through with them the more concrete the ideas became. I am deeply indebted to them all and, in particular, the open minds and open hearts with which they received all I had to say, including my personal experiences which I relayed to them also.

Key among them is Dr Emmanuel Okoro. We have worked and researched together for a number of years and his instant excitement for the material I presented to him helped me shape it a great deal. Dr Diana Anchescu brought her own wisdom to my musings and, through the discussions we had, made me ever more grateful to have her as a deputy. The characteristic enthusiasm and authentic openness with which Dr Ben Smith – head of psychology in the organization where I work – received the material also spurred me on to take the next steps, and I continue to enjoy very much our ongoing research relationship as we explore new treatment ideas that stem from this perspective. Another research partner and fellow traveller is Dr Lisa Woods and her vantage, combining mindfulness with a detailed knowledge of statistics and research methodology, has been and continues to be invaluable to me.

Yet another crucial colleague is Mirabai Swingler, the chaplain on my ward, with whom I have enjoyed more enlightening discussions about the nature of my field than almost anyone else in it. Working across both the spiritual and psychological realms she seems almost effortlessly to combine the two in her understanding of things, and in sharing this with me has helped me do the same.

No acknowledgement of any of my books could ever be complete, however, without mention of my inde-fatigable agent, Doreen Montgomery. With her many years of experience of the publishing world she always helps me to mould my final manuscript in a way that is beneficial to all, and her straight-talking style makes for an excellent and highly productive working relation-ship. As we often say to one another, we really do make a good team.

Finally, the people who deserve the most thanks are those who keep me grounded in between: Maria, 'the boys' (Owen and Kieran), my sister and, of course, my dear parents whose love and kindness towards me truly knows no bounds, and whose wisdom has always formed the backbone of all my endeavours.

References

Chapter 2

Mark Epstein, *Going on Being* (Wisdom Publications, 2001)

Chapter 3

Eknath Easwaran, *Dhammapada* (Nilgiri Press, 1985)
Adyashanti, *The End of Your World* (Sounds True, 2008)

Chapter 4

Russ Harris, *ACT Made Simple* (New Harbinger
   Publications, 2009)
Gina Lake, *Radiance* (New Satsang Foundation, 2006)

Chapter 5

Jeffrey Schwartz & Sharon Begley, *The Mind and the Brain*
   (Harper Collins, 2002)
Fritjof Capra, *The Tao of Physics* (Flamingo, 1975)
Vlatko Vedral, 'In from the cold' (*New Scientist*, 13
   October 2012)
Bruce Rosenblum & Fred Kuttner, *Quantum Enigma*
   (Duckworth Overlook, 2007)
David Bohm, *Wholeness and the Implicate Order* (Routledge
   & Kegan Paul, 1980)

References

Fred Wolf, *Dr Quantum's Little Book of Big Ideas* (Moment Point Press, 2005)
Rupert Sheldrake, *The Science Delusion* (Hodder & Stoughton, 2012)
Mario Beauregard, *Brain Wars* (Harper One, 2012)

Chapter 6

Nahid Angha, *Principles of Sufism* (Jain Publishing, 1991)
Eknath Easwaran, *The Upanishads* (Nilgiri Press, 1987)
Eknath Easwaran, *Dhammapada* (Nilgiri Press, 1985)
Stephen Mitchell, *Tao Te Ching* (Harper Collins, 1988)

Chapter 7

Adyashanti, *The End of Your World* (Sounds True, 2008)
Mark Epstein, *Going on Being* (Wisdom Publications, 2001)
William James, *The Varieties of Religious Experience* (Digireads.com Publishing, 2011)
Mario Beauregard, *Brain Wars* (Harper One, 2012)
John Hick, *The Fifth Dimension* (Oneworld, 1999)

Chapter 8

Dawn Baker et al., 'Depersonalisation disorder: clinical features of 204 cases' (*British Journal of Psychiatry*, 2003, 182, 428–33)
Carol W Berman, MD, 'Out of his body: a case of depersonalization disorder' (*Huffington Post*, 9 November 2011)

Chapter 9

S Friedman, L Smith, D Fogel, et al., 'The incidence and influence of early traumatic life events in patients with panic disorder: a comparison with other psychiatric outpatients' (*Journal of Anxiety Disorders*, 2002, 16(3), 2 59–72)

References

D P Chapman, et al., 'Adverse childhood experiences and the risk of depressive disorders in adulthood' (*Journal of Affective Disorders*, 15 October 2004, 82(2), 217–25)

Marc-Alain Descamps, 'Spirituality of Depression' (*The International Journal of Transpersonal Studies*, 2003, Volume 22, 84–5)

Dr Edward Whitney, 'Personal accounts: mania as spiritual emergency' (*Psychiatric Services*, Vol. 49, No. 12, 1998)

Chapter 10

Mark Epstein, *Going on Being* (Wisdom Publications, 2001)

William Stillman, *Autism and the God Connection* (Sourcebooks, 2006)

Chapter 11

Adyashanti, *End of Your World* (Sounds True, 2008)

Pim van Lommel, *Consciousness beyond Life: The Science of the Near-Death Experience* (HarperCollins, 2010)

Chapter 12

Roy Porter, *Madness: A Brief History* (Oxford University Press, 2002)

E C Johnstone, C Freeman & A K Zealley, *Companion to Psychiatric Studies* (Churchill Livingstone, 1998)

Pat Bracken et al., 'Psychiatry beyond the current paradigm' (*British Journal of Psychiatry*, 2012, 201, 430–4)

Jeffrey Schwartz and Sharon Begley, *The Mind and the Brain* (Harper Collins, 2002)

Eugene S Paykel, 'Cognitive therapy in relapse prevention in depression' (*The International Journal of Neuropsychopharmacology*, 2007, 131–6)

David Kingdon, et al., 'When standard Cognitive Behavioural Therapy is not enough' (*The Psychiatrist*, 2007, 31: 121–3)

Mario Beauregard, *Brain Wars* (Harper One, 2012)

References

Rupert Sheldrake, *The Science Delusion* (Hodder & Stoughton, 2012)

M Brooks, 'Anomalies: 13 things that don't make sense' (*New Scientist*, 19-25 March 2005)

Rita Carter, *Mapping the Mind* (Phoenix, 2010)

Jim Holt, *Why Does the World Exist? One Man's Quest for the Big Answer* (Profile Books, 2012)

David H Rosmarin, et al., 'A test of faith in God and treatment: the relationship of belief in God to psychiatric treatment outcomes' (*Journal of Affective Disorders*, Vol. 146, 3, 25 April 2013, 441-6)

Russell E Phillips III, et al., 'God's will, God's punishment, or God's limitations? Religious coping strategies reported by young adults living with serious mental illness' (*Journal of Clinical Psychology*, Vol. 63, 6, June 2007, 529-40)

Steven A Rogers, et al., 'Religious coping among those with persistent mental illness' (*International Journal for the Psychology of Religion*, Vol. 12, 3, 2002)

Rosemarie McCabe and Stefan Priebe, 'The therapeutic relationship in the treatment of severe mental illness: a review of methods and findings' (*International Journal of Social Psychiatry*, Vol. 50, 2, June 2004, 115-28)

Chapter 13

Pema Chodron, *The Places that Scare You* (Element, 2003)

Mario Beauregard, *Brain Wars* (Harper One, 2012)

Mark Allen, et al., 'Participants' experiences of Mindfulness-Based Cognitive Therapy' (*Behavioural and Cognitive Psychotherapy Journal*, 2009, 413-30)

Pema Chodron, *The Wisdom of No Escape* (Element, 2001)

Candace Pert, *Molecules of Emotion; Why You Feel the Way You Feel* (Simon & Schuster, 2012)

Index

Index

Index

Index